Prais
The Revolution

"The world is shifting with a rapid and increasing pace of change that is complex even for adults. The need to transform education is crucial for our children to be prepared for this new world and their future. *The Revolution* addresses this need by sharing how we can embrace learning that can be messy, and even a little bit crazy. Ellwein and McCoy, middle school principals, are passionate about how and why they make this happen for their students. The authors weave in stories and examples, challenges to begin unlearning in order to relearn, points to ponder, and suggestions for revolution@ry work. *The Revolution* is a compelling call for all of our schools to change—and to do what children need *now*."

—**Barbara Bray**
author, speaker, blogger, and host of the *Rethinking Learning* podcast

"A child-centered revolution is waiting to begin from within these pages. When it comes to empowering learners, this manifesto doesn't pull any punches. The authors write from a place of deep credibility and anchor their aspirational message in very real terms. This book will be a juggernaut in leading school change."

—**Brad Gustafson, EdD**
award-winning principal, author, and speaker

"This book is the key to moving middle schools into the twenty-first century and out of the stone ages of educational tradition! The four descriptors of the 'New Middle School Learners' were spot on as I have witnessed this very real transformation of our learners from my eighteen years of educational experience. I'm recommending this book to all educators who are risk-takers who are willing to face the challenges of preparing the next generation of leaders through a revolution of instructional delivery and student engagement!

Great job, Derek and Darren. Thanks for the support and the plan of action to guide us to sustainable success for our students and the communities we serve!"

—**Derrick O. Dalton (@derrick22dalton), EdS**
middle and high school transformational principal

"Darren and Derek share the vision of what schools should be for our students in *The Revolution*. They give us glimpses of how education can be relevant for every student in the classroom by encouraging us to move past outdated practices and provide a future-thinking, students-centered educational experience.

The Revolution shows educators a path toward building the schools our students deserve."

—**Todd Bloch (@blocht574)**
seventh-grade science teacher and #mschat founder

"Darren Ellwein and Derek McCoy have written a must-read book for anyone wanting to #BecomeBetter and improve their practice. Read and learn alongside many educators, just like yourself, who are ready for the education revolution."

—**Melanie Farrell (@MelanieCFarrell)**
digital learning coordinator, Wake County Public Schools

"Immensely practical, *The Revolution* will challenge you to take your school on a journey to the next level of relevance and empowerment. Filled with powerful stories and new ideas, you'll be given the tools to create authentic learning, develop compelling spaces, and foster outstanding relationships. I couldn't put it down. It's amazing to see what's possible when learners are given opportunities to take greater ownership of learning."

—**David Geurin (@DavidGeurin)**
author of *Future Driven,* award-winning principal,
and international keynote speaker

"Derek and Darren hit it out of the park! Throughout the book they provide you with their insight into the culture of learning in revolutionary schools and make you rethink what school should be. They push you to think differently about how we create learning environments and provide learning opportunities for the learners—both students and teachers—in our schools. I guarantee you will pause, reflect, and then implement at least one of their ideas the day after you read their book."

—**Jay Posick (@posickj)**
principal, Merton Intermediate School

"If you are looking to be part of a revolution that will impact you as an educator and, more importantly, make a greater impact on your students, then *The Revolution* by Darren Ellwein and Derek McCoy is the book you've been waiting for. Filled with practical examples and personal anecdotes, this book will push you to reimagine how schools can look for all learners."

—Jimmy Casas
educator, author, and speaker

"Darren Ellwein and Derek McCoy have produced a powerful book about educational transformation. Drawing from personal experiences as middle school principals who have led revolutions in their own contexts, Darren and Derek provide an honest account of the joy, the struggle, the moral mandate, and the challenges of revolutionizing education to better serve all children. But this book is more than personal tales. It includes wonderful insights, practical strategies, and friendly guidance for anyone who wants to transform education from top-down knowledge transmission to a student-driven journey of discovery."

—Yong Zhao
Foundation Distinguished Professor, University of Kansas,
and author of *Reach for Greatness: Personalizable Education for All Children*

"In *The Revolution,* Darren and Derek challenge all of us to move out of our comfort zones and take risks as educators and leaders! The call to action is to lead with grit and compassion and to develop a culture of empowerment and collaboration in every school. I pray that we answer the call soon, as our students will need us to be courageous! Start the revolution now!"

—Salome Thomas-EL
award-winning principal, author, and speaker

*Special thanks to
Bethany Smith (@bethanyvsmith)
for her revolution@ry visuals.*

THE
REVOLUTION!

IT'S TIME TO EMPOWER CHANGE IN OUR SCHOOLS

DARREN ELLWEIN
AND DEREK L. McCOY

The Revolution
© 2019 by Darren Ellwein and Derek L. McCoy

This book is available at special discounts when purchased in quantity for use as premiums, promotions, fundraisers, or for educational use. For inquiries and details, contact the publisher at books@daveburgessconsulting.com.

Published by Dave Burgess Consulting, Inc.
San Diego, CA
daveburgessconsulting.com

Cover Design by Genesis Kohler
Editing and Interior Design by My Writers' Connection

Library of Congress Control Number: 2019901898
Paperback ISBN: 978-1-949595-26-0
Ebook ISBN: 978-1-949595-27-7

First Printing: March 2019

DEDICATION

First, we want to recognize our God for bringing people in our path to grow our journey. We believe bringing our work and friendship together was His work.

Second, we dedicate this book to our families.

> Darren—Having kids that are three, nine, and twelve meant I had some sacrifices to make so that I could make them number one while working on this book. Thank you to my wife for understanding the times I had to be involved in this project when the family was in the crazy cycle. I love you all.

> Derek—Gary and Imari, you both are inspirations and drivers for what I do. I know God blessed me with you to make me strive to be a better man, father, and educator. To my brothers and sisters, you guys keep me uplifted!

Third, we want to dedicate this book to our staff: teachers, custodians, kitchen staff, and other assistants in our buildings.

Darren—A revolution cannot happen with one person. The family of teachers at South Middle School have been the epitome of flexible thinking and risk-taking. You have made a vision a reality and are an example for schools around the world. A special thank you to Jim Holbeck, my superintendent, for providing the flexibility and trust so our learners can be empowered.

Derek—It took a lot of courage for the West Rowan Middle staff to take the multiple steps of faith and risk that helped transform the school. While I know I'm grateful, I'm positive the learners thank you—remember this was for them.

Fourth, our friends and PLN members. You guys rock!

Dave and Shelley—thanks for letting us fly the #tlap flag!

And finally to our parents. Thank you.

Darren—I think of my father who created and maintained a simple life for his family in rural South Dakota. This book is dedicated to him. What he accomplished with just an eighth grade education, never ceases to amaze me. My dad was proof of resilience even when an education system said he was not meeting its standard. Dad, you are a hero to me, and I now see the innovations you were creating daily on the farm and at the bowling alley.

Derek—My parents had a simple mission for their ten kids: Be good people and go to school beyond high school. We grew up in rural Georgia with many obstacles, but we never had excuses. This book and our degrees and drive and love of God, are for you both.

CONTENT

PREFACE

WE BELIEVE THAT THE education system—at every level—is in desperate need of a revolution. With that in mind, this book is our manifesto. With it, we hope to incite the kind of change that will provide better, more relevant opportunities for students in schools everywhere.

Why is change a necessity? Because the world has progressed. All around us, industries leap forward in terms of technology, innovation, and productivity, while the education system clings to structures that were created more than seventy years ago. Society has moved beyond the Industrial Revolution. It does not need a workforce of laborers for industry as it did in the twentieth century. It does not need a work-force in cubicles. It does not need leaders who hold an unyielding grip on tradition.

The most important reason for this revolution is our students. Most of the education world believes instructors should drive the teaching without learner input, but we believe learners should be included in decisions that affect their education—and their future. If this revolution in education is going to be successful, we must rid ourselves of the "sage on the stage" mentality. And to do that, we have to trust that our learners are capable of creating the future.

Derek and I (Darren) have come to realize that our lives have much in common. We are both principals at the middle school level. Both of our schools have students ranging from upper-elementary age to high school ready. They are both stages of significant transition, and our work as principals allows us to understand these worlds to an extent. We hope this book will show you how working with and growing kids in our respective contexts drives our passion to innovate the structures and supports of our schools.

While there are some obvious differences between Derek and me, our family backgrounds are also strangely similar. Farming is an important part of both our lives. Derek is from rural Georgia, and I still farm in South Dakota. The landscapes and weather vary, but our experiences are the same. We both have a strong work ethic thanks to parents who drove themselves into the ground laboring every day. We both place a strong emphasis on faith in God and the neighborly kindness that encompasses rural America. We both have a powerful connection to the land and what it produces. We both understand the importance of being able to use a unique and innovative skill set with few resources.

I have learned that education cannot meet the needs of every student. My father was a young boy during the Great Depression. He attended a country school because he had to, and his experiences with school were mixed. I recently found his sixth-grade report card—his grades were not very impressive. He wanted to quit school in favor of working on the farm, but by law, he couldn't drop out until completion of his eighth-grade year.

My father died in March of 2016. He suffered from Lewy body Dementia, and if he hadn't been ill, he would have spent his last days on the farm. It was the piece of land on which he was born. Literally. After my father completed the eighth grade in the late 1940s, he had the option to leave school, and he did just that. School had no relevance to his passion for farming or his dream of building a bowling alley. His decision not to complete high school weighed on him emotionally at times. He would make comments about "not being smart" because he did not continue a formal education. Hold on to that phrase, "formal education."

As I reflect on my father's life, I see the innovative traits he possessed that the school system could not recognize or address. Formal education in post-World War II society tried to force students to fit into predetermined boxes. My dad did not fit in those boxes. I am aware that he needed some basic skills to function in daily life, and he certainly felt the same way. But my father is like thousands, maybe millions, of students today who feel like they don't fit the system.

If you are wondering if he accomplished his goals, he did. During the day, he was a dairy farmer and grew corn and soybeans. This was something he loved to do. He was also highly skilled at fixing machinery with very few resources. His childhood poverty had taught him to never throw away anything that might be useful again—especially equipment or parts. To see him find a chain, sprocket, or running gear from unused equipment was fascinating. I didn't realize as a young boy just how innovative he was.

What about the bowling alley? He fulfilled that dream as well. With only an eighth-grade education, my father not only started a business but organized the construction of the entire structure. He ordered railroad cars full of cement bags to mix the foundation. He asked people in the community to help bring in each bowling lane. The newspaper covered the event in 1961. I hadn't yet been born, but the photos I saw later brought the story to life for me.

I want you to think about formal education today. Does our education system force students to fit its parameters? Who should drive an education—the student or the system? What will it take to revolutionize our education system so that it addresses the needs of each learner who walks our halls?

We believe a revolution has begun at a small scale. Educators are beginning to see the need for change as they witness students giving up on their education and dropping out. Kids are asking us to make their education relevant to their lives because they don't feel like they fit the system they are in. Teachers want to be more than curricular robots. They want their jobs to have value; they crave the chance to create. Revolution is stirring, but more revolution@ries are needed to facilitate change. We see it happening in our schools. You will read about real revolutions at Harrisburg South Middle School in South Dakota, my South Family. Derek will tell you about the revolution from his previous school in North Carolina and the changes that took place during the three years leading up to his move back home to Georgia in 2018. The following chapters and words will not only speak of this revolution, but they will also show you how it's unfolding.

For us, this revolution starts in the middle.

#revoltLAP (revolt Like A Pirate)

INTRODUCTION

ONE OF THE MANY blessings of my (Derek) professional life was being asked to give a co-keynote address in 2015 at the American Middle Level Educators Conference in Austin with my good friend John Bernia (@MrBernia). Being asked to speak was a humbling experience, but sharing the stage with a good friend as we discussed our excitement about middle schools was as emotionally overwhelming as the energy from the crowd. Sharing this moment with thousands of people who loved middle school as much as we did was a once-in-a-lifetime moment.

On my return trip home, I struck up a conversation with a woman at the airport while we were waiting to get screened. I won't forget this day. We were making the typical waiting-in-line-at-the-airport small talk. At some point she asked me why I was in Austin, and I told her I was a middle school principal and had been in town for a middle school conference. I'll never forget her reaction and tone. It went from light curiosity to flat, dry humor as she said, "God bless you because I couldn't deal with all those middle schoolers." If you have been a middle school educator for years like I have, you have no doubt heard this same reaction. Like I've done so many times before, I offered her my usual responses: "I hear you" and "It's not that bad."

After leaving the screening area, the exchange lingered in my mind. I'd had a great time at the conference, so why did I respond to that woman the way I did? Why did I laugh at her derision?

Here is a fact—I love middle school.

I truly can't see myself working at another level. I loved my time as a middle school reading and math teacher because it helped me be a better parent. I loved my time as curriculum coach and assistant principal because I knew I was making a difference with a fun age group. Now I have another great job I am extremely proud of—middle school principal. I work with great educators and students who are learning about themselves, growing their independence, and finding their places in the world. Why was I making light of this awesome role and institution? I was dishonoring the very people John and I had just spoken to at the conference.

Not long after that trip to Austin, I embarked on a mission to change some of those general misconceptions about middle school and share the profound improvements happening right now in the areas of middle school teaching and learning.

I can't tell you how great it's been to work beside Darren on this project. Not only have we become great friends, but we also sync on two main points:

1. We believe that the systems and practices of middle school [and all of K–16] that we have inherited from past generations aren't doing our learners, teachers, community, or our world any good. Industrial age education doesn't work in an information age.

2. We believe it's time for a revolution. Great things are happening at the middle school level:

   - Learners are choosing their learning paths.
   - Students are engaging in global conversations about things that will absolutely be part of their future.
   - Middle school learners can advocate for themselves and for topics they are passionate about.
   - Teachers are challenging students to be creative and innovative in how they think about and solve problems.
   - We are empowering students in settings and with resources that will not only challenge them to reach new levels, but will also give them the space and freedom to be as creative as they need to be.

In this book we are going to share the work we do in our schools that is changing and challenging education, particularly middle school education. We are going to share how innovative teaching, technological integration and enhancements, personalized learning, and the evolving role of educators and other leaders are reshaping how our middle school learners are succeeding. We are also going to challenge you to rethink what is being done at your schools and inside your classrooms!

Our hope is that the fear and apprehension our parents and community members have about middle schools will be replaced with an admiration for the incredible transformations that are happening there and an urgency to create learning environments that will help schools produce generations of problem solvers and activists that will change THEIR world. We hope that all of K–12 will be inspired to take a critical look at the "whats" and "hows" we guard so closely in our schools to determine if they're reflecting the "why" of education. As George Couros writes, "It's no longer about compliance, it's about empowerment." We want to empower schools to become vital learning hubs where middle schoolers grow and succeed.

It's on us to make sure the work, actions, and productions of our learners and educators are relevant, meaningful, and known to the world. We must let the world know we are proud. We must be willing to change what we value most about learning and learners so we can not only reimagine school at every level, but also lay the foundation for a revolution that will produce the schools our students deserve.

#revoltlap

CHAPTER 1

THE TRUE REVOLUTION@RIES

*Don't wait for the perfect moment,
take a moment and make it perfect.*
—Aryn Kyle

*L*IKE MOST EDUCATORS, OUR experience as students led us to this great profession. The entertaining and knowledgeable teachers we had growing up provided us with some memorable classroom experiences, and those memories drive us to create that same kind of learning environment for our own students. Even our not-so-great teachers served as examples by showing us what not to do in the classroom.

My (Derek) middle school experience happened more than thirty years ago in a small, rural town in Georgia. It was a model of textbook classrooms:

- Desks in rows, perfectly aligned
- Teacher's desk immaculate and separate (remember those old-school brown planners?)
- Students arranged by last name or grade
- Quiet
- Chalkboards in the front
- Learning meant giving the right answers, reciting definitions, or spelling words correctly
- Textbooks were the curriculum
- Teacher-driven classes
- Regimented classes with fixed grading
- Homework was always a couple of pages in the textbooks (and if you were lucky, you could find the answers in the back)

Our days were pretty standard and designed to be that way day after day, year after year. It was a measure of success—teacher standing at the front of the classroom, students facing forward and working quietly while following the teacher's instructions to the letter. Success was measured by compliance and reduced noise levels. In our small community, my teachers knew me because they had taught my family members and because my mother worked as a professional. But I think it's safe to say they didn't know the real me—how much I needed to move, how I liked to socialize, how I disliked drawing and handwriting, and how competitive I was. They didn't really know how I learned. In most of our classes, the teacher would tell a story or make a presentation or offer a demonstration, and we would watch from our seats. Independent research was limited to reading the textbook pages the teacher assigned, completing the work, and waiting on our grade to indicate whether or not we learned something.

This isn't criticism. Our teachers did the best they could with the resources they had at the time. And more importantly, they were good people implementing systems and practices they learned from others that were the agreed-upon best strategies at the time. The one-room schoolhouse mindset is powerful and deeply embedded in our society and what we believe about education. That model focused on control and work completion. There have always been those who believe learning is different from what we practice in schools, but it has been hard for that belief to take root. Unless we are on a mission to unlearn the trappings of our traditional educational experiences, we are doomed to repeat and reinforce this cycle.

Back to my own experience. In our school we had an 'A' class and a 'B' class, and they were exactly what they sound like. Once in them, students could not move out or change groups. Regardless of maturity or progress over time, once a student was labeled, that was it. It's not a stretch to say that our present tendency to label or separate some students from others is a carryover from those days. How do you see it in your school? Is the teaching in those classes equitable? Is there any flexibility for students who may blossom later than others or have the benefit of a teacher who fires them up? Are all students getting an equal shot at all levels of opportunity or learning? We once called this tracking, but whatever name we place on it, it means the same thing— some get more than others.

Rectifying this has become a mission of ours. I was fortunate to have had one parent who worked in my school and fought hard to keep her active son out of remedial classes at the urging of teachers. My mother still fondly talks about her fight to keep me from being tested for remedial classes. To her credit, in the third grade our school got its first gifted teacher who also tested all students, and once she tested me, she validated my mom's thoughts with a simple statement all progressive educators are familiar with: you all aren't teaching him how he needs to be taught. It turns out I loved to read anything about Greek and Roman mythology and loved to talk about it!

I want to state plainly here that I am not bashing my teachers. I loved them for what they committed to do every day, and they genuinely loved me. They came to school to make a difference for us, to be a difference. The women in my small rural town knew that if they didn't commit to educating us, it wouldn't happen. We loved them for what they did.

But it does lead to some reflection points: Why did you decide to become a teacher? Was your goal to duplicate the learning experience you had when you were in school? Are you looking to give your students the same middle school experience you had?

If you're like me, someone who attended middle school thirty years ago, the answer is probably an emphatic "No!" Not only because they don't make film strip projectors anymore, but also because you have a strong conviction that much of your own middle school experience should not be repeated or held up as a best practice. There is much room for improvement. Now apply that thought to your elementary, high school, or collegiate experience—would you want to give that same experience to your students? Would you want that same experience for your own children?

Every Revolution Needs a Good Teacher

Take a look around your classroom and/or school and reflect on your answer. Do you see practices and results that reflect your answer? Darren and I had to admit that we didn't see them in our own schools.

I became an educator after a heart-to-heart with my former wife. It took a good, frank talk to help me put some cold, hard facts on the table about my pursuit of a graduate degree in political theory. The most important fact? I absolutely wasn't passionate about it.

The only jobs I had enjoyed had been in college when I tutored students in math in non-traditional settings that allowed us to fill in gaps and have good conversations.

If I were to work with students in a classroom, where could I have the most fun and impact? The clear answer for me was in a math classroom, not in a political science classroom.

Although those talks happened more than twenty years ago, I remember them like we had them yesterday. I remember sharing with my wife about two of my high school teachers who were great influences in my life. One of those teachers was Mr. Stubbs, my tenth-grade geometry teacher. Back in the day, we taught geometry with proofs (a lost art form), so not only did you have to know math, but you also had to be able to articulate the process, especially when there was a problem on the board. Mr. Stubbs was a great teacher—he was funny, knowledgeable about math, and he took time to know his students well. He made the uncomfortable work of doing math proofs in front of the class fun, describing it as creating a feeling of "elation." When I reflect on Mr. Stubbs' class, my memories are primarily positive. In his classroom, I felt entertained, I felt smart, I knew I belonged there, and I actually learned a great deal. That kind of classroom, I told my wife, was what I wanted to create.

When my wife, Fatima, and I talked, we didn't make a list of qualities for my ideal classroom, but if we had, I think it would have looked something like this:

- A fun, inviting learning environment
- Challenging curriculum
- Lots of laughter and talks with friends

Think about your list. Why did you become a teacher? If you are in a different role, why did you choose that role? Why are you a principal? Instructional Coach? Department Chair?

Now the Rub

Darren and I became fast friends and project partners because as we talked more about middle schools today, our personal and familial educational journeys, and K–12 learning environments in general, we developed a theory: educators aren't remembering their lists.

At the end of this chapter, we're going to ask you to share your list, so be ready. For now, however, we want to dive deeper into the spirit of the list. What's the underlying message of an educator's list? Think of this as your mission in life for working with learners. Try to remember what your thoughts were when you began your commitment to serve learners.

What's on your list?

A Look at Now

We're going to offer two points as challenges for you:

- Does your classroom or school look how you want it to? Is it in its ideal form?
- Does your classroom or school feature a learner-centered or teacher-centered design?

While we know most educators put a lot of thought into designing their learning environments, many of those same educators overlook powerful and simple modifications that can make these same environments more fun and engaging for learning. Unfortunately, this oversight is often the result of a distrust in our learners that has been handed down in, or even beaten into, our professional schema.

As educators we've been conditioned to believe it's the safer and better practice to assume the worst is just around the corner, especially if we don't plan for every possible problem in the classroom. Any hint of student flexibility is dangerous, so we're expected to keep a tight control. And the same goes for the parents of our students, most of whom think a safe, productive classroom is desks in rows and a strong, skillful teacher who demonstrates and lectures. In some schools where I've worked, strong and skillful equates to domineering and stern. That is simply not the case. It's the revolution@ry leader in the room who makes the difference.

Control vs. Trust: Old-School Classroom Management

How many times have you heard a colleague say, "I teach my subject, but it's up to the students to get it"? If you've heard this before, chances are it's from a teacher who focuses on delivery and content and not on learners or assessing understanding. If protecting how we cover content is the priority, then we will likely see several things:

- A heightened protection of whole-group instruction

- Lots of teacher talk and a need for quiet
- Moving all students to the next topic regardless of what assessments show
- A fixation on rigid classroom management

We want to be clear here: these elements are important, but it's how we implement them and how they support learners and the deep understanding of content that is most important.

So our mission is simple: start a movement wherein we champion a revolution in education!

Many of the things we value and think are the most important in school are things we have inherited through the years and become very accustomed to. As a result, we have associated school with these traditions. We spend a lot of time building up these systems and practices (e.g., the school schedule, covering content, rigid behavioral expectations for learning environments), and our intense focus on these areas has made us beholden to them to the extent that we prioritize them over what matters most in our schools.

But these systems and practices aren't on our lists. They aren't what we were passionate about when we decided to become educators or what gave us sleepless nights before our first day of school! These practices and beliefs aren't the fires in our bellies that have us rushing to school every day looking to be a difference for students, and they definitely aren't helping us produce more eager learners.

What Do We Do?

Our purpose in writing this book is to get back to what originally fired us up about learning and teaching and working with learners. It's that simple. We want you to keep your most important reasons in the forefront, always taking time to ask yourself, *Why did I want to be an educator?* and *How did I want to inspire students?*

When you think about your day and what you spend the most time doing, how much time do you devote to your list of most important items? Consider the old adage, "What we think, we become." It certainly applies to teaching. What educators spend their time thinking about directly impacts how they interact with learners and co-workers. If you're spending the majority of your time thinking about policies and schedules and standards instead of investing in the students themselves, how can you ever hope to instill in them a love of learning?

We didn't become educators to enforce rules—we wanted to make the best kind of difference.

We didn't become educators to manage a schedule—we wanted to make sure learners were achieving and growing every day.

Many of us have simply lost sight of our why. Thanks to conventional teacher-prep, mentoring from an old-school mindset, and years of traditional "schooling," some educators have never had a real grasp on the needs of the learners in their charge. Just like my childhood teachers, they know some facts about their students but not how they learn and think and process information. Our focus has too often been placed on the classroom instead of the people inside it, on classroom management instead of classroom culture, on teaching methods instead of the learners we're teaching. We've all had countless discussions about how students learn in different ways, but have we committed to developing new ways to measure learning?

In the conversations we had leading up to writing this book, our greatest motivator was the work we are both doing in our middle schools. Middle schools don't get the love typically shown to other schools. Don't get us wrong—we get some good support, but not at the level of many other schools, and we are the neediest group.

We believe most people are projecting their own fears when they disparage middle school kids as "out-of-control" and "hormonal" and "difficult." Too often critics want to impose extra rules on these adolescents out of fear of what could go wrong instead of looking at all the potential for good that exists in our middle schools.

This is why we are calling for a revolution and why we will be referring to you—the ones who have made the decision to pump your fists and acknowledge that change has to happen—as revolution@ries. This movement will be fueled by the resources and networking abilities we have in our society today.

Let's embrace our learner-centered movement.

Revolution@ries See Learners

In our schools, you will find revolution@ries who want things to be different because they know our students deserve and need someone who understands learner needs. Revolution@ries embrace alternatives because every learner needs something different. I (Derek) think about my own kids, Gary and Imari, and how we had to take different approaches to teaching them to read and learn in their formative years. When it came time for kindergarten, Gary needed a caring teacher who set high standards for his empathy and character, because he came into kindergarten as a strong reader, while Imari did well with a no-nonsense, goal-driven nurturer. Different learners have different needs, and revolution@ries accept that.

Revolution@ries Use Their Spaces

Revolution@ries don't limit themselves to the traditional use of spaces—they see opportunities! They can completely reimagine their learning spaces by bringing in more color to stimulate creativity in the middle school brain (How's that for contradictory thinking?), tearing down walls, removing lockers, and making changes to give students space to do revolution@ry work!

We're going to share stories about how some middle school educators are empowering middle school learners through personalized learning and relevant, rigorous experiences, and how the different spaces play a critical role in creating opportunities to empower learners. Bean bags, lawn chairs, coffee tables, and high chairs provide more than a different aesthetic—they give flexible minds a physical landscape that encourages them to be all they can imagine being.

We're going to share some great examples of how revolution@ary educators are embracing different paths and different ways of thinking to get out of the traditional trappings of "how we do school."

REVOLUTION@ARY IDEA

How are you being intentional about setting a stage for learners to share their stories?

It's Time for a Revolution!

We think you picked up this book for two reasons: 1) you want to start a revolution where you are, and 2) you want to see what other revolution@ries are doing. It goes without saying that a reimagined middle school won't happen unless we reimagine the role of the teacher. In this book, we want to focus on shifting our thinking and language towards learning and learners. Something as simple as changing a title can be the start of adopting this new approach to changing lives.

My own K–12 experience has permanently imprinted in my mind that students are passive, compliant, and waiting for the teacher to give directions. In most of my classrooms, the teachers were great people who cared about their students. They were great storytellers. They had to be. It was a different time and age for our teachers. But today, revolution@ries want learners to be the storytellers. Revolution@ries don't want to be the sage on the stage—they want learners to build their own platforms and share their inventions, stories, and dreams with the world.

Revolution@ries empower learners by allowing them to create and innovate in any number of ways:

- Produce writing that can be shared globally and receive feedback from any device around the world
- Record videos to start dialogues with other learners in the classroom, school, or around the world
- Explore their interests and have the space and opportunity to consume
- Create content in a way that best fits their learning styles
- Use unique ways of demonstrating mastery of concepts

Given this glimpse into what revolution@ry work involves, are you satisfied with your title of teacher? If you are already doing revolution@ry things for your learners, we encourage you to continue that great work and possibly find inspiration and new ideas in this book. But if you aren't satisfied, we hope you will question how things can be different and explore new opportunities. We hope you see the need to shift your understanding of what students do in our schools and begin questioning what empowered learners can do. We hope you want to question the traditional understanding of teacher and embrace the role of facilitator and designer. After all, you aren't the gatekeeper of all knowledge, doling out information to students working quietly in desks arranged in perfect rows. That was the classroom of thirty, forty, even fifty years ago. Today's classroom should look vastly different. This is your moment to decide to do it differently, to do better for your learners.

Revolution@ry Facts

When you look at revolutions in history, you see people who committed to social and political change. They committed to difficult talks and actions to bring about a real transformation. And it is a risk. While there won't be life-or-death risk here, there is significant risk to changing our fundamental educational beliefs, thoughts, and practices. That kind of change can feel personal and threatening. Remember when you decided to switch from regular soda to diet soda? It was tough, impacting various parts of your day and leaving you mildly disappointed or irritated, but it was totally survivable. Remember when you gave up soda altogether? Now that was a life-altering change, a fundamental shift in how you chose to hydrate your body. What about the first time you integrated technology into a lesson in your classroom? Fundamental shift. Or the first time you differentiated your students' learning activities? Another fundamental shift. None of the changes were entirely comfortable, but you made the effort and commitment and followed through, reaping great rewards as a result.

Revolution@ries don't shy away from these big changes. They size up the risk and step forward with hope and confidence. Here are a few more truths we have come to understand about revolution@ries:

Revolution@ry Fact #1:
They embrace different skill sets.

Revolution@ries are educators who:
- Listen with empathy
- Motivate others
- Move beyond polite conversation to authentic relationships
- Take risks and abandon safe practices
- Embrace relevancy, particularly in the area of instruction

Revolution@ry Fact #2:
They build fantastic cultures
in their learning environments.

The term "classroom management" holds us back. It leaves us trapped in a time when we valued quiet and control over everything else. Some educators still hold quiet and control as prerequisites for a dynamic classroom—but that certainly isn't the case. Have you ever met a teacher who uses statements such as "My classroom always has noise" as justification and assurance that learning is taking place even if you hear learners moving around inside? When teachers make this statement they are giving an excuse for noise in the classroom. That's a shame. We should not have to excuse activity in the classroom like movement or talking or not sitting, and we definitely shouldn't have to explain it as a part of the learning process. We should all have the expectation and belief that activity in the classroom is necessary and a critical component of the dynamic learning experience. Let's not make excuses, let's design active learning.

REVOLUTION@ARY ACTION

Embrace the fact that your teacher desk can be a significant barrier between you and your students, and then get rid of it.

One of the revolution@ries I've (Derek) had the pleasure of working with is Justin Owens (@MrOwens_Math). In addition to the great work he's done with gamification and personalization (we'll explore that later), he and I have had several conversations about barriers and divisions in the classroom. He describes the strong desire he has developed over the years to help teachers "tear down the fourth wall" in classrooms. He refers to the very real barrier teachers can establish between themselves and their learners from behind their desks.

Don't set out to manage your classroom or keep students at arm's length. Dive deep into your educator toolbox and build genuine relationships with your students. Let them know you know them and care about them and that you are excited they are in your classroom. If you visit Justin's room, you are very likely to see him standing on tables yelling, "Dilly Dilly!" and waiting for a like response from his students.

Nothing beats passion and building relationships. Relationships first! This means engaging in real, intentional work—not just saying that you like what you teach or that you care about your students.

Does your passion for your work come out in the projects your students have in front of them? How would your students answer this question? Does the culture in your environment inspire and motivate?

Revolution@ry Fact #3:
They accept that the work
will be as rewarding as it is tough.

In this book, we're going to talk about our mindsets, what middle school learners can do, and about redefining our spaces, work, and expectations for our middle school learners and education in general. Some of this won't be new and some will have a different spin, especially as we talk about middle school (#itstartsinthemiddle). But we are going to ask you to embrace the unfamiliarity as we think differently, and to give up some things for the benefit of elevating learners.

This should be a collaborative learning experience. We are encouraging you to join our discussions at #revoltlap and grow your understandings while building up your PLN (personal learn-ing network).

This is the start of your Revolution.

For us, it starts in the middle.

We all will learn and grow.

CALL TO ACTION

▶ In what ways would you say your teaching (or leadership) practices are revolution@ary?

▶ What fears do you have about changing old habits and methods?

▶ Whom do you consider a revolution@ary teacher?

▶ Get your highlighter and Post-It flags ready to mark ideas you find in this book!

CHAPTER 2

ADD SOME REVOLUTION TO YOUR MINDSET

The biggest risk you take in life is not doing something.

—Naveen Jain

IF WE, AS REVOLUTION@ARY educators, are going to cause a real shift with ideas like those presented in this book, we must have the right mindset. The grit required to sustain this movement will be considerable. (For our purposes, we are defining grit as "a belief in an idea or principle that requires persistence through resistance.") Make no mistake—the traditions of the past will work against us. The outdated habits of not only teachers in the trenches but also school district leaders will work against us. Our own fears might also tear us down, *if* we allow them. To stay the course, we must continually remind ourselves of the cost—to our kids—of doing nothing. We must embrace a total sea of change. Yes, this is bona fide revolution!

We realize most of the educators reading this will be teachers. Our hope is that every school leader will read this, but the truth is that most of our powerful difference-makers are teachers. Real change comes from the teachers in the classroom who put it in place. Leaders present a vision, and teachers make it happen. Use your voice to work with your leaders. Do you feel like your voice is being heard at your school? Is your input on your school's purpose valued by those in charge?

Before revolution@ries can do what is best for the students at their schools, they must have a clear purpose to rally behind. This purpose usually has more traction if it is a collective belief, widely supported across your entire school community. In this chapter, we want to guide you through finding your purpose as a group to create dramatic change. We want to inspire you to band together to create a revolution.

Finding a Collective Purpose

Picture this familiar scene: The start of the school year is fast approaching, and you will have several days of in-service or professional development before students arrive. What will that PD look like for you?

Far too many PD hours are spent with logistical material and protocol minutia. If your experience is similar to that of my (Darren's) school five years ago, then you spent this precious time reviewing the staff or student handbooks, discussing district protocols, or catching people up to speed on new policies. Sure, there is a time and place for these items, but your primary focus should be on building a unified culture. You can always count on one thing: positive changes don't happen in an unhealthy culture.

Culture is the most important aspect of any school, so our focus must be on creating a culture where our learners will thrive.

It took me a while to figure out just how important creating culture is—and that we need to talk and learn about how to create it. A few years ago, I spent our few PD hours doing what had always been done: going over handbooks, policy, and special notes from central office. By the time we had finished all the managerial items, the teachers were stressed out and anxious to get on with planning for their learners. The amount of information educators have to try to ingest can become an impossible mission at times.

A Shift in Our First Hours Together

Harrisburg South Middle School (HSMS) is a part of a rapidly-growing district in South Dakota. It is nestled just below Sioux Falls along Interstates 29 and 90. South Dakota has been my home since birth. I have great pride in my state. I have great pride in my school district and building. This pride comes from its outlook to the future and its willingness to question tradition and embrace change. Embracing change is hard for some groups of people, though.

HSMS, I believe, values change because we realize it is best for kids. The staff has embraced the voice of the learner, implemented a personalized learning model, created a vibrant makerspace, and connected learning with schools around the world. We are not a private or charter school, although people often ask me if we are. We are a public school in an incredible district that embraces a vision for what education can be.

How does a group of individuals build a foundation on collective purpose? Collective purpose thrives when the culture is open. Teachers must feel like their voices matter and be treated like the adults and professionals they are.

I was tired of relaying tedious information to my teachers. We all want value in our time, so I set out to find that value.

What changed for me? First, I followed the footsteps of a few great teachers in my building and flipped the instruction of our meetings. We are all adults, so I wanted to treat them like adults, trusting them to learn on their own. Links to handbooks or recorded explanations of policies were sent to them to review.

Second, it hit me that we needed to have a defined purpose, a collective purpose. Our building had to focus on our purpose for our learners. Producing a collective culture is difficult without a purpose to hang on to. I believe it is so important to have a cohesive understanding of why we do what we do. Ask yourself what is more important: the tradition or the purpose?

But we were still moving and working without a purpose, and this led to a moment of clarity. With my presentation ready, I invited all our staff, including aides, custodians, and office staff, to be present for this building meeting and professional development day. I started with a quote from *Bold School* author Weston Kieschnick (@wes_kieschnick): "There are two types of schools: Those that prepare kids for the future, and those that allow adults to live comfortably in the past."

I explained that I wasn't there to make them comfortable. Preparing kids for the future was our real work, and I was there to push them to transform learning.

I challenged them to transform and push one another to create something that hasn't yet been achieved.

HSMS had already begun to move the needle toward innovative practices. There were a lot of traditional practices in place that had adults at the center of the learning process, but the voice of the learner was becoming more prominent. Our learners were creating unique projects. Teachers had started to use their freedom to experiment with new practices. Our makerspace and personalized learning culture were growing. Now we needed to bring it all under one purpose.

REVOLUTION@ARY REFLECTION

"There are two types of schools: Those that prepare kids for the future, and those that allow adults to live comfortably in the past."

—Bold School **author**
Weston Kieschnick (@wes_kieschnick)

Personally, I had begun to feel the power of change when kids had a voice in their products and a choice in their learning. My own motivation for learning grew as my vision for learning expanded. No longer was I learning with blinders on: follow this curriculum, do this project the same time each year, do the same as the person next door. A renaissance had taken hold, and I wanted that to be understood by all the adults in the building.

Rita Pierson has given one of the most watched TED Talks in the education genre. Her focus was on relationships and the power of believing in our kids. I wanted her passion to awaken a revolution. After showing the Rita Pierson TED Talk (Search YouTube for Every Kid Needs a Champion), our staff met in grade-level teams to brainstorm the question, "What is our purpose at Harrisburg South Middle School (HSMS)?" To gather their ideas, I had them write their thoughts on Padlet, a tech tool that works as an online bulletin board. Asking for their input gave them a voice in determining our purpose. When this was completed, I told everyone that we needed to build this together. They had some great answers listed in the Padlet, but I challenged them to keep digging deeper. What drives us to be the best? What one thing pushes our purpose? Someone eventually said the one word that would become the glue that held our work together—relationships. Our purpose would be building relationships.

REVOLUTION@ARY REFLECTION

Fill in the blanks:

Our staff's focus is

_____

Our students want

_____

Our parents need

_____

The lesson here for educators in all fields—K–12 and higher education—is to be open and vulnerable with one another to discover your true purpose. What would those in your learning environment say is your purpose? Does everyone agree on what the most important things are about your school? Shifting the culture won't happen until there is understanding, buy-in, and belief! If we are going to reimagine and rebuild our learning institutions, it's going to take real work.

Next, I told them that every program, idea, and instructional strategy had to align with this purpose. For example, we have a program called iChoose, a combination of Edcamp for middle school learners and Passion Projects. I asked the teachers if this fit our purpose of building relationships. The answer was yes. As we were planning our personalized learning model, I asked if this program fit our purpose. Another yes. Any new programs or ideas after this point would have to fit our purpose of building relationships. Probably the greatest change came in our language. We were very intentional in our use of the word "relationship." It is very common now to hear the word used in our classes and in daily discussions. It has become a valued signpost for the culture of our building.

So why is this important? What's the goal of finding a shared purpose? To answer this, think about the change our learners experience on a frequent basis. The change can be social, emotional, physical, or related to culture, home, disability, or gender. With so many changes in their lives, it is vital that we have a common purpose and consistent atmosphere for them.

REVOLUTION@ARY IDEA

We can't settle for a common vision and mission. There must be shared beliefs, mindsets, and values. We can support the vision of all students succeeding, but what about truly believing that all students can succeed? A vision and mission statement alone won't ensure we all work as hard as we can to help every student succeed. Changing our culture will require changing beliefs, skills, and mindsets to empower learners.

Developing a Growth Mindset

During the process of finding our purpose, we discovered that we were moving toward a growth mindset for all of us—students and staff alike. Teachers searched for and collected resources that helped them teach "soft skills" to learners—skills that would help change the culture of our school.

With the amount of change we were looking to create at HSMS, we needed to emphasize optimism and the ability to learn from challenging situations. The journey to change education requires keeping the vision for change while trudging through the messiness of learning. It requires focus.

HSMS discovered that we were moving toward the pillar of establishing a growth mindset. It was an integral part of our journey. We were determined that our growth mindset would be more than an impressive buzzword—that wouldn't serve our learners in any way. We resolved, as a school, to weave growth—and all that entails—into our language, practices, interactions, and lessons. Most importantly, we shared our growth mindset with our students. We let them know up front that growth is about moving forward, progressing, changing, and improving, not necessarily about reaching a particular goal or grade. Growth should be continuous.

In the classroom, that meant sometimes recognizing effort over accomplishment. In the book *Mindsets in the Classroom,* Mary Ricci discusses the concept of growth versus grades. Each year, we complete a book study as a staff, and we wanted a book about growth mindset. This book was fitting for what our staff was learning at the time. Schools are too hung up on grades as the end-all-be-all. Grades have the tendency to focus us on an end result. But what about the process for getting there? What about those learners who did not earn an A but improved their learning by an incredible amount? This is the effort piece of a growth mindset.

On a personal note, I have a son on an Individualized Education Plan (IEP). Thank goodness I have grasped hold of Carol Dweck's work on growth mindset, because I now know that my son can improve his learning status. It is not fixed. I constantly emphasize the importance of hard work because I know I need to push him to believe in his work ethic. Millions of kids today are led to believe they cannot grow their intelligence. They give up, drop out, quit. We need to emphasize hard work and diligence in a task. My son loves school to the point where we can't keep him home during the summer. Even though it is hard and takes him longer to complete assignments, we continue to emphasize hard work. Growth mindset.

At HSMS we dove into the Genius Hour movement in 2014. It started with a few staff testing out the concept in their classes. I had my eighth-grade staff ask if they could take one day per week to complete Genius Hour projects. I had seen individual rooms do this, but not entire grades. What was the next step? We planned what it would look like. With no guide for us to follow from another school, staff planned the steps and system needed for kids to create projects. Growth mindset.

What was my thought? This is fantastic! It was the type of concept and movement I wanted educators to embrace. A few weeks later, I had the seventh-grade team of teachers ask to create Genius Hour projects. Finally, the sixth-grade team decided to do more of an Edcamp formula once a week. Developing a new concept at this scale went against the mindset of many staff in my building. Several had to work hard to maintain optimism because there were tough trials during this time. But it is the resolve that rises from the trial. Even though this Genius Hour idea has evolved into something different, it set the stage for staff to view things differently.

I do want to note that growth mindset is not just optimism. Being overly positive will not win the major battles of our day. You need to combine optimism with a resolve to fight for what you believe is best for learning and instruction. That's how you create a structure that fosters growth.

Kids have learned the importance of social learning and strive for acceptance in their new setting. Our job is to replace the emphasis on acceptance with values that are less about popularity and more about work and passion.

Growth mindset is more than being optimistic. It requires action and planning. It is risk-taking with the grit to persevere. Where do you group yourself in relation to these traits?

REVOLUTION@ARY REFLECTION

Our school has systems in place that encourage students to work through adversity.

YES or No (Explain)

Students have practiced how to work through a problem independently.

YES or No (Explain)

Students have learned to shed the learned helplessness label.

YES or No (Explain)

Staff take instructional risks for their learners.

YES or No (Explain)

Staff understand grit and promote it with their learners.

YES or No (Explain)

Most learners carry the heavy load of emotional baggage with them to school. As educators, we might be among the few people in their lives providing optimism and hope on a daily basis. With that reality in mind, equipping and encouraging our learners must be intentional work. Our calling as educators is much more complex than people outside of education understand. And it takes years for some educators to understand the gravity and importance of their decision to accept the responsibility of leading a classroom or school. Our responsibility is not about worksheets or workbooks: it's about growing our students.

A growth mindset not only provides learners with a direction, but it also drives our daily desire to encourage persistence and perseverance. Surround yourself with others that have that growth mindset, because you will need the support during the marathon of a school year.

Naveen Jain is an entrepreneur with an off-the-charts growth mindset. He grew up in India in a family with few resources. Despite this hardship, he found a way to come to the United States and has become very successful. One reason I gravitate toward his work and quotes is his positive outlook on life. In addition to being a positive thinker, he is presently working on a project for making moon travel a common experience. He explains his philosophy about the half-full, half-empty glass debate. To paraphrase his comments from an interview on the podcast *Inside Quest,* he could not care less if you believe the glass is half-full or half-empty. He only wants to know if you are willing to fill the glass! This is the charge presented to my staff recently. If you are agreeing on the purpose of building relationships, iChoose, personalized learning, etc., I just want to know you are going to "fill the glass." Imagine a staff that would all "fill the glass" of the learning culture at your school. Here's to glasses that are overflowing.

Empowering Mindsets

Three years prior to discovering our purpose as a staff, I presented five pillars, or mindsets, to push our instructional culture. I wondered what would result from a group of educators with a collective purpose believing in core mindsets. It is so important to allow our teachers flexibility to be creative. For HSMS there were five empowering mindsets we focused on. They are:

- Risk-Taking and Learning from Failure
- Technology and Social Media
- Voice and Choice
- Creation and Innovation
- Collaboration

Risk-Taking and Learning from Failure

Risk-taking requires an open environment where risks can be taken instructionally. Revolutions are sparked by risk-takers, people willing to move against traditional currents. In our opinion change is needed in education, but in order to see change, you need to possess a willingness to take risks.

At HSMS we wanted to blend a student Edcamp model with Passion (Genius Hour) Projects. We called the project iChoose to exemplify the power of kids making choices based on their interests. I would be lying if I told you that all our staff were onboard with this. Implementing this program was a risk because I was asking staff to depart from the usual routine/schedule and give up some instructional time. After listening to feedback and cycling through several iterations, we now have kids leading sessions. This result would not have been possible unless people agreed to take a risk.

Risk requires a certain amount of freedom for educators. People need to feel and see safety when they're attempting something outside traditional routines. Leaders need to communicate freedom and flexibility. Leaders also need to make their risk-taking visible in our classrooms. We can choose if we want to allow the textbook or the learners to dictate the outcomes. A traditional classroom has the safety of the textbook and a prescribed scope and sequence, but the outcomes fall short of authentic learning at times. Since educators are accustomed to this safety, it can be hard to leave the safe zone. There has to be a communication of, "Hey, I want you to take this risk even though the idea could fail."

What about our learners, the kids in our classrooms? For our learners, we sometimes need to break years of training that taught them not to take risks. They have been told to sit, listen, and work. Many times the "work" has no value to them. This model represents a top-down mentality of control. But control can be shared. It scares some educators to death, but they can give freedom to their learners and still maintain control of their classrooms.

A by-product of risk-taking is failure. Why? Because when you risk, you are typically trying something that has never been tested before. Allow your instinct to take over during these internal therapy sessions! There will always be the pull to just do the safe thing. But we want to encourage you to live, to see our educational world as more than ordinary.

"We learn from failure, not success" . . . "Never let failure get to your heart" . . . "Failure is not fatal." These are just a few common quotes about failure. Many of the quotes you search don't even make sense with how we understand failure. In my view, failure is a place to visit, but I won't stay there. If you read the preface, you learned about my dad. He had to overcome many biases because he stopped his education at grade eight. His gift was making something out of nothing. There were countless times a machine would break down, and he would walk to the tree grove for help. There in the trees lay a graveyard of out-of-use machinery, and he would harvest their parts to fix a failure. Failure on the farm or the bowling alley led to learning. But when he was at school, failure led to ridicule and discouragement.

What image does failure resemble in your classroom or building?

Teachers

The worries for practitioners when it comes to instructional failure are scope and sequence—meeting all the standards by the end of the school year. Many people fear job loss if they fail to meet tradition.

Risk will include failure. If you allow risk-taking, you need to have the correct mindset of failure. Punishment shouldn't follow failure, yet that is a reality in many schools today. Perfection is not possible, but growth is possible. Open the doors to learning: Failure is learning.

Failure is a part of the creative process. Following a set curriculum from a textbook has no allowance for a creative process. Robots can dictate a textbook with assignments. Revolution@ry teachers embrace the joy of creating. By their example, they inspire innovation. Have fun with your work!

Learners

Our learners fail constantly in our makerspace at HSMS. In this space they feel safe to risk and fail. Failure can spark creative problem solving. The best products from our learners have iterations. Place a trademark within your spaces for feedback loops, a routine of reflecting on the problem and finding better solutions. We even build this idea into some of our courses. The iterative process requires that you learn from your mistakes. In the end, don't we just want learners to produce the best product possible? We must help them understand that the most important goal is creating the best possible product, not meeting the due date or making the grade. Shift that mindset to help them work toward an outcome they will be proud of.

In our makerspace, I have seen our learners harvest a fan from an old computer tower and a motor from an automated hand-towel dispenser, attach them to a cardboard structure, and end up with a creation that doesn't move. An amazing build-up led to an anti-climactic result. After receiving feedback, they added items to their design. The kids wasted no time problem solving and eventually built a working boat. They are living the iterative process.

This approach can begin the process of building the capacity for a universal culture trait. Working where the entire building has a growth mindset is an amazing experience. We know because we are experiencing it. The risk-taking conversations have filtered down to our learners. They are understanding that failure is not the evil. Quitting when failure emerges is the evil.

Technology and Social Media

Technology is an important tool that can help produce revolution@ry change when properly put to work. For HSMS, I can't imagine the scale of our changes without iPads, our scheduling software (personalizedlearningtools.com), and other applications. Technology should make our work more effective and efficient. It should enhance learning opportunities by giving options not available with print resources. If it does not, then it is being used incorrectly. We need to put our fear of technology behind us and see the potential it has to enhance learning.

Another method to find growth is social media. Twitter houses one of the largest professional networks of educators. Typical traits of these educators are: a willingness to share, risk-taking, an I-will-help-you mentality, and idea generation. Since we've connected with these educators on Twitter, our professional growth is off the charts. Many of our ideas have come from our professional learning network on Twitter. Don't wait another day to get connected and grow yourself.

We know the usual fixed-mindset constraints: time, negative publicity of social media, and the learning curve of the software. Find someone who has already taken the step to guide you through the process and reveal the benefits.

Voice and Choice

Allow learners a voice in their work and a choice in programming. If teachers feel the freedom to risk, they are given a voice in how they instruct. And there is another trickle-down effect to learners. Providing voice and choice in their learning opens so many doors. Find ways to make the learning co-driven. Voice and choice can take place in formative and summative assessment. Allow kids to make choices about how they can complete mastery or display their learning. First, you need to let go of the traditional chapter test format for a summative test. Second, you need to tune in to their creativity. Each learner is different and will display their work in their own unique way, if you allow them. Top-Down (Control) vs. Voice and Choice. Free yourself from doing everything for them. They can take the reins of their learning, and the results will be more authentic for them. Our personalized learning model in chapter ten is a perfect example of voice and choice for kids.

Creativity and Innovation

I don't believe leaders focus enough on encouraging teachers to be creative in their work. A majority of schools rely heavily on purchased curricula or creating inflexible pacing charts that dictate when learning should occur. I am not recommending that we do away with curriculum entirely; novice teachers need some tools as they plan and prepare. But relying solely on your curriculum does not promote creativity. Educators need to be trusted to make curricular decisions that are current to our learners.

In 2018, John Delle (@themrdelle) decided to gamify his English/language arts (ELA) sections at HSMS. What did he need? He needed a clear view of his standards, pieces of curriculum, people to connect with who have done this, and freedom to make it happen. He needed permission to be creative and innovate the content. He created a battle board for a fictitious world that was all related to ELA. The results have been positive and empowering.

When voice and choice are present, learners can produce content that is original and valuable. Their creativity is limitless if we allow them a space to think. Too many educators tell kids what to do, how to do it, and hold tightly to control. They practically do all the thinking for them. This approach creates compliant versus creative kids.

Let's revisit John Delle's classroom. He has taken several pauses along the way to gain feedback from his learners. In one instance, he decided to create a template only to find out that a learner had created it for him. On another occasion, he allowed kids freedom to reinvent the spaces (his classroom) to fit the content they were learning. As John said to me one day, "The best ideas I have in my room are student-created." We need to move past our perception that adults are the only holders of ideas and knowledge. I have seen our kids create innovative mastery projects when they can choose how to prove their mastery.

REVOLUTION@ARY REFLECTION

How do you convince your leaders to allow you the creativity you need?

Collaboration

Learning is not solitary, yet we create islands and silos in our buildings. We claim a space as our room or a curriculum as our work. It is so important to maintain a collaborative spirit for our learning as adults. At HSMS we try to find purposeful ways to collaborate. Our teams will spend time discussing their content with one another and seek avenues to dovetail their work or, as we call it, cross-pollinate our content. We also have built-in time where each teacher has to visit a colleague's classroom at least once a month. Even when we collaborate as teams, we intentionally foster collaboration by sitting together in a tight circle. We want to be able to see one another and speak TO one another.

Technology has allowed us to collaborate virtually. Derek and I are both Digital Principal of the Year recipients and value collaborating with "colleagues" around the world. The importance of having someone at your fingertips who can inspire or build your learning cannot be overrated. We need pushers in our lives to keep us moving in our learning. What do you want from a growth perspective? I really believe we need pushers to continue our professional growth. The end product is newness, energy, and growth.

"Pusher" is the term I created to describe those that push my learning. Pushers make you revolution@ry! Pushers grow your work and inspire you to be better. They share an idea, strategy, design, or quote that makes you better. Do you have pushers in your school? Or maybe I should ask, Do you seek out pushers? Every school has a rockstar educator, so make a connection with them and find more pushers on social media.

Pushers don't have to be a virtual connection on social media. My close friend Travis Lape (@travislape) is one of my top ten pushers! I am fortunate he is in my district, but even if he wasn't, we would still be connecting on Twitter. He is a juggernaut of knowledge and willingly helps people all over the world. Again, most of my pushers are virtual, and it opens the door to so many possibilities in our world today. Motivational speaker Billionaire P.A. (@BillionairePA) has an amazing story of going from humble beginnings to self-made millionaire. He is known for his "Speaking Dreams into Existence" messages. He has a quote I modified: "You are the sum of your five closest friends." In education I tell people: "Show me your five closest professional-learning contacts, and I will show you your future in EDU." Connecting with those that push your learning is so crucial.

At HSMS I encourage teachers to have a Twitter account for professional use. The connections to teachers outside our building, authors, and companies create many growth opportunities. For example, if we need an idea on producing TED Talks with our learners, I know the experts to contact on Twitter or other social media sources. Many times I will connect with a variety of scientists in the plastic pollution arena to speak with our kids who are doing projects. This type of collaboration grows adults and kids.

Whom would you include as pushers in your professional growth?

CALL TO ACTION

▶ How would you define the purpose in your classroom, school, and/or district?

▶ Think about your mindset regarding education and your students. What do you need to do to develop a Revolution@ry Mindset?

▶ Which of the five pillars in this chapter is a strength? Which pillar(s) require you to take risks?

▶ Explain what you are doing to grow your learning. Who are the "pushers" in your professional growth?

CHAPTER 3

REVOLUTION@RY LEARNING SPACES

PASSION! REVOLUTION@RIES HAVE IT. Passion is a word used often in life and hopefully inside your school. My (Darren) definition of passion is "an interest that drives an idea to reality, even through trials." Exploring your passion doesn't feel like work. Passions are joy, and they have the potential to bring a cause to fulfillment. Derek and I share a passion, and it's one we love to pursue at our respective schools. We have an ever-growing passion for innovating learning spaces.

My passion for spaces launched at Stanford's d.school in Palo Alto, California. After seeing their philosophy on flexible, dynamic spaces and furniture, I had the opportunity to speak with Scott Doorley, lead designer of the school. I used this experience to evaluate my school (more on this later in the chapter). I push my staff to break traditions, like rows of desks and maintaining sterile environments. Most rooms in our building will have foam cubes, whiteboard tables that mimic a coffee house setting, and simple Craigslist additions like a sofa or dorm chairs. Later in this chapter, you will read about the Stanford-inspired designs we build in our school.

Think back to your own middle school classroom. What did it look like? What image do you have in your mind?

Rethink the design of your learning space. You should include your students in this process. The "way it has been done" is not working for a majority of our students. This "way" requires a room with desks in rows for the purpose of producing compliance. You cannot empower learning with traditional rows. Warning: if you head down the road to redesigning and rethinking spaces, you will meet resistance. You will hear, "Why can't we just have rows of desks for learning?" or "What benefit is there to changing what we have always done?" We encourage you to be persistent, smile, and prove them wrong.

Be revolution@ry!

Revitalize and Refresh

Think of the school where you work or the schools your children attend. They likely have classrooms using the traditional desks-in-straight-rows concept. This structure has long been thought to give teachers maximum results and control. Arranging chairs and desks this way is all about achieving compliance.

It's also straight-up boring. Think about it—in this format, innovation is limited to shuffling the seating chart each quarter! Where's the fun? Where's the creativity? Where's the freedom?

Consider your own home. How often do you change the sofa-loveseat configuration in the living room just because you are tired of it? Every year? Every three years? When was the last time you changed the color of one of the rooms in your home? Why did you do it? What were you hoping to achieve? How did the new color make you feel?

When my (Darren) wife asks my thoughts on a paint color in our home or a new piece of furniture, I typically don't have a preference. My response is, "Looks good to me" or "I guess that works." I work best when there is a blank slate. For example, we have a space under our stairs where we store toys, my old comic books, and other misfit items. I love moving everything out once a year so I can reimagine the packing of the space. It is actually a game to see how much free space I can create, the Rubik's Cube of storage spaces.

We need these changes to happen. More specifically, our brains need these changes to happen to keep our moods and creativity on a positive upswing. When we walk into a freshly-redecorated room, we immediately appreciate the transition from past to present. This transition keeps us revitalized and fresh. With this reality in mind, we ask our revolution@ry question: How can a space redesign benefit our middle school learners?

Spaces That Evolve and Empower

A challenging issue for many educators is determining whether or not their space fits the needs of all of their learners. The building I inherited consists of rooms with a standard square footage, so I have traditional spaces like most of you. I want to encourage you, though, to think innovatively with that space. Remember, our kids, no matter what grade level, need empowered learning that takes place in diverse learning environments.

The design of a space should evolve daily based on the learning needs of your kids. Even the newest and most innovative spaces being built today are still just spaces unless educators tailor the confines to their students' learning needs. The reality is that most of us are teaching in traditional box-like classrooms. For reasons beyond my understanding, school business managers and district leaders are also still purchasing traditional seating. The desks might be newly built, but the style screams 1960s. Our central offices are providing our schools with items that fit a decades-old mindset.

On top of clinging to tradition, most school districts aren't discussing the science of learning spaces. And it is a science. The typical coursework at universities consists of pedagogy and methodology for particular emphases or content related to education. A research study published in 2016 revealed positive outcomes of a learning environment with nontraditional classroom design. The study indicates that flexibility and student ownership have positive results in subject areas with increased anxiety, such as math.

d.school Inspiration

In response to the urging of some educators in my professional learning network on Twitter, I (Darren) had a team from my school apply to The Hasso Plattner Institute of Design at Stanford University. The d.school, as it's known, is a prime example of changing a space to fit the needs of learners, even higher education learners. This old building on the Stanford University campus is transformed inside. It has design concepts that encourage flexibility and multidimensional use. In one area of the building, you can create the space you need by using wall jacks and large whiteboards. It also has creative signage and studios dubbed Teaching+Learning, Experiments, and Environments Collaborative.

After applying to the d.school, our team from HSMS was accepted to participate in the Design Thinking Process workshop. As we were learning about the five tiles of Design Thinking (chapter 6), I was enamored with the design of the spaces! An open space with wall jacks and whiteboard tiles to create your needed collaborative space is great, but how can that fit a K–12 setting? A sofa on casters that can be moved from one area to another is a cool concept, but how does it fit K–12? A room that was wall-to-wall whiteboards? A vehicle with a transformed interior space for reading? No relevance to K–12? Keep reading and give it a chance.

During breaks, I took pictures and interviewed Stanford students, taking every opportunity I could to learn about the purposes behind their spaces and furniture. I learned that Stanford students had the flexibility to create the size of their spaces in the second-level learning area. They were empowered. I learned that each space had a specific name that captured the essence of the learning that would take place there.

When our team returned to South Dakota, I put all these ideas from Stanford on paper. Here was my first takeaway: every inch of my building had to be evaluated for use. My advice for you: take some time and assess how many square feet in your school are wasted because they're not being utilized to their full potential. The best time to do this is without learners or adults in the building. Take a walk. Take notes. Have someone with a design mind walk with you.

Another piece of advice is to observe the spaces while learning is taking place. When I returned from Stanford, the first thing I did was walk my building, many times. I took notes on our used and unused areas. I assessed the approximate number of minutes an area was utilized, if it was utilized at all. When I found an area with potential for learning, I sought feedback from those that would use it. That feedback included learner feedback. This is not about "comfort to lose engagement." It is about empowering kids to learn in a manner they view as best for their learning.

REVOLUTION@ARY ACTION

**Evaluate every inch of space
—every hallway, closet, and empty classroom—
as a potential learning space.**

A third piece of advice is to speak to staff who want to test the creation or concept of new spaces. Find someone who wants a new challenge or who embraces risk-taking. Sit down together and view the learning that takes place, and then plan the space to fit the learning. I could tell you our approach and the names of our spaces, but you need to make this your own. Inspiration is plentiful if you search Twitter hashtags or Pinterest tiles. Here are a few to check out:

- #flexibleseating
- #rethink_learning
- #rethinkinghomework
- #rethinkschool
- #igniteyourSHINE
- #flexiblespaces
- Pinterest: search "plywood seating", "school seating", "DYI school seating"

The final advice involves the learner. Consider those who will use the space to determine the maximum potential. You can get their feedback and ideas by using a Google Form or other data tools, but there is no substitute for that one-on-one conversation. I highly recommend getting feedback while learners are using the space. I also recommend allowing learners to name and own the space.

The Learning Spaces Revolution at West Rowan Middle School

One of the earliest changes to happen at West Rowan Middle School (WRMS) was prompted by a tweet from Shonda Hairston (@PrinHairston), the principal of a nearby elementary school. Shonda and her team had renovated some common spaces for teachers and students. These spaces were redecorated with comfortable furniture and featured a college theme to inspire students. The overall vibe made it easy for teachers and students to decompress, talk, and relax. Tricia Hester (@trish_hester), our assistant principal, rushed to me (Derek) after seeing the tweet with an idea to bring this change to WRMS. After a team collaboration, we came up with a design challenge for all three grade levels and our exploratory classes. Our awesome PTA cooperated and gave $500 to each group for supplies, paint, and decor. Our requirements were simple—try anything and everything! At the end of the nine weeks, our groups came up with some spectacularly unique ideas for each empty classroom on each hallway. Ideas and supplies ranged from standard paint and magnetic paint to lawn benches and pallets for seating. We also recycled old school furniture. In the end we had learning spaces that were truly centered on our learners, offering flexible furniture, whiteboards, and open spaces for movement and collaboration. There was tremendous pride in our completed work. Visitors would commend the teachers for their hard work and comment on how lucky our students were to have such great spaces to work in.

With our new spaces in place, we used our core values of having compassionate leaders who communicate and collaborate with integrity and purpose to evaluate the work we were assigning to our learners. We wanted to make sure there were high levels of work for students to collaborate on and complete—compelling work for compelling spaces. Creating these spaces with our driving purposes in mind helped us frame questions and conversations about student engagement and levels of creativity.

Helper Hubs

After we returned from Stanford's d.school, HSMS staff began to create spaces with our learners, and together we created Helper Hubs in the hallways. Before we went to Stanford, the hallways in my building were underutilized spaces designated for students who were in trouble or needed to complete late work. Maybe your school uses its hallways for the same purposes. But why should these spaces represent a penalty box when they could be a place where learning happens? (A quick thought on penalty boxes: We all have kids who don't mind the penalty box. The hallway, or any space that is set aside for the purpose of isolation, is a good space to get out of work.) At our school, we decided to reclaim these spaces and give them a new image and design. Rather than penalty boxes, our hallways are now empowered learning spaces.

At South Middle School, we decided to use hallway spaces for personal learning time. We planned to norm these hallway areas early in the year with input from our kids, empowering them to create structures for learning. What we didn't anticipate, however, was their idea for a hallway space called Helper Hub. The idea started when a few of our learners were working individually on a project and realized they also needed a learning space to help their peers. It is one thing to work in a personal, quiet area, but how can you reject an idea fostering collaboration? Helper Hubs became the solution.

One of the first questions school leaders ask when we talk about our Helper Hubs is, "What about supervision?" I (Darren) don't disagree that our learners need supervision, but as Derek says regarding many areas of our work, we can't live in fear. To manage the use of Helper Hubs, when students request to use the space, they must provide a game plan for learning. They are also asked to show evidence of that learning when they're finished.

To take this a step further, we have parents, educators, and professors visiting our school on a regular basis. When our visitors and

I walk past one of our homemade whiteboard tables in the hallway, I stop and explain the learning purpose of the environment with our visitors. But if the kids are in the hallway, I let them do the talking, and they seldom disappoint. The evidence of learner empowerment is the voice of our students. It becomes more valuable to hear it from kids because they are living and creating it.

On one occasion, I had a group of educators touring the personalized learning models in our building. We passed a Helping Hub location where two learners were using the whiteboard tabletop to draft some writing prompts, and two others were completing a grammar exercise. As we walked by, I asked if any of them wanted to explain the purpose of Helper Hub. One of them, a sixth grader, began explaining that the purpose is for her to provide help to other learners in this space. She then displayed a real-time example of this as she was working with her friend. Our visitors left the space impressed by two things: the space created by kids and the explanation from the student. This is the perfect example of fostering learner empowerment in the design and norming of spaces.

Let's rethink the spaces in our school. Rather than following traditional practices, let's consider how we might repurpose any of the spaces in our schools to address learners' needs. If hallways can become spaces where students produce their best work (rather than places for isolation), how might other spaces in our schools be used?

At WRMS, hallways have become a more accessible and requested space for our students to work in. Both our schools are 1:1 with iPads. Derek's second year at WRMS marked the district's third year with iPads. One tradition took a critical hit: lockers. The need for lockers was greatly diminished, if not eliminated, by the shift to 1:1. We decided to remove lockers from each of the hallways, and with the help of an industrious agriculture teacher, Tim Burns, the school installed "genius bars." Each genius bar holds two whiteboards and markers, a narrow bar-height table surface for students to complete assignments, and stools for sitting. The decision to ditch the lockers so we could create personalized, optional spaces for students just made sense. Seeing students over the years develop a strong desire to move to open spaces in order to communicate and collaborate on assignments was very fulfilling and rewarding. Moving and working in an unconventional way is a powerful draw for learning.

These revolution@ry shifts were about learner needs. Uprooting and disrupting school traditions and systems had to happen to embrace learner needs.

I (Derek) am often asked about the cost of revamping our hallways with genius bars. If the lockers in your school are like those at West Rowan Middle, then there are only about ten bolts that are holding them in place. We worked with our district maintenance to take them down. While we got lucky with paint (our hallways were scheduled to be painted that summer), trust me when I tell you I was ready to take three hours to paint these new genius spaces. The only expenditure was on whiteboards and the tables we attached to the walls (thanks Mr. Burns, WRMS Ag Teacher #1). These renovations provide a great "friendraising" opportunity for a staff or community member to help with the school. The end product is space where students can work, create, and collaborate.

How Do I Begin?

As you consider how to create new, unique learning spaces for your students, keep these key points in mind:

Time—It takes time to evaluate spaces. Rely on people to help your thought processes. When I have teachers who change their spaces, it can take anywhere from minutes to hours to change the landscape of the room. When kids are involved, it takes longer, but you reap greater rewards in the end.

Help—Whom do you ask for help when you begin changing learning spaces? I like to pull in several different perspectives, from teachers to contractors to designers. Chances are, your colleagues have unique insights or talents that will help the process. Ask people. Work to elicit their input about your ideas.

Permission—Each building and district has different protocols for furniture and painting. Check with the "powers that be" to see what limitations might be present. If you have limited power to change a space, gather research to support your ideas. You can also show them examples like our (Derek's and Darren's) schools.

Start Small—I will be honest—I don't like to start small, but I will recommend you begin with a small space. Empower the learners and teachers in your school to choose this space and design it (remember, this book is about empowerment). I would also start with the space in your classroom and the hallway outside your room. Some of you will have a cove or open area to dream with as well.

Key Questions

Think about these key questions before, during, and after your design.
- What is the purpose of this space?
- How will my kids learn in this space?
- What is expected of learners in this learning space?
- Whom do I ask for permission with this project?
- Who in my PLN can I ask for help or ideas?
- What parents are able to help with design ideas, resources, or funding? It never hurts to ask! You will also have parents with resources from the community to assist you.

A Learner-Centered Culture

After our staff and learners had a voice in utilizing the hallway space at HSMS, we were very intentional about using it for individual or group work. The benefits? Movement, privacy for work, the option to stand or sit, collaboration, and greenscreen opportunities. What did we miss from that list? The reaction from our kids—they LOVE using the hallways. They are empowered to modify the space to fit their learning.

Another favorite for our learners involves using nooks and foyers. These are popular areas for creativity, and it is common to see green paper on the walls for green screen projects. Groups appreciate having a space that seems like a private studio to plan or present. Instead of wasting time walking to the library to use the green screen, they can modify the space close to their classroom or studio.

Individual learners like the extra privacy to read or complete work for an artifact in these spaces as well. I love that they understand how they learn and can advocate for their learning. If they need a space to finish their podcast, they initiate the conversation with our facilitators. How do we maintain order in these spaces? The learners. They were involved in the norming of the spaces, and that has brought about genuine empowerment.

The Emotional Impact of Space

Before we move to the next thought, I (Darren) want to build on the empathy of the user. How difficult is the power struggle inside you right now? How hard is it to give up control of your work? Let me make a farming analogy. Every spring I can't wait to begin preparing the ground for planting. I can control the tractor, equipment, and supplies and make sure they're ready to go. What is out of my control? The weather. I might think the ground is dry enough to till, but the ground could be like a sponge and cause the tractor to get stuck. Picture being stuck in our work, which typically includes our students. You can control the curriculum, create the behavior plan of expectations, and assign work. You cannot, however, control each student or how they will act or react in your planned environment, and they are less likely to react positively if they do not have an emotional connection to the space.

Think about a space that makes you feel relaxed. For me it is my bed at home. I stay in a lot of hotel rooms, but I never sleep as well as I do in my own bed. My bed was customized with my input on the size and firmness, and the store allowed me to test a variety of mattresses to find my preference. Then they made the bed to fit me. I literally have an emotional connection to my bed.

How about another example? While writing this chapter, I was in San Diego. I had recently left South Dakota, which was covered in a blanket of snow and had temperatures ranging from ten to forty degrees below zero. To energize my writing, I sought out some California sunshine. The locals thought it was strange that I wanted to write outside by the pool, but the sun and the sixty-degree temperature were life-giving!

Let's transition back to education. Do your spaces have an emotional value for your students? Is your classroom just another room in a building full of similar spaces? Do learners look forward to being there? If not, know that it doesn't have to be that way. Emotional connection to a space happens when kids have voice and choice and are empowered to create. The space becomes internalized. Can you feel that last statement? When learning can be internalized, productivity increases and creativity blooms.

I recently delivered new furniture to a classroom. It was just a few Hoki stools that allowed for some movement. Emily asked if they were for her classroom. She then began redesigning her classroom with these new stools in the layout. She also decided to move the whiteboard table from the hallway into the classroom. Did I mention Emily is a sixth grader? It is her studio, her classroom. She and her classmates have an emotional connection with their spaces; the spaces have become internalized. The teacher, Maria Pettinger, has developed a control structure in her room that is more than democratic. It has family values.

Emily and her classmates have been empowered to control their learning space. And why not? Why would we ever design a learning space without the learner's input? It is time to revolutionize our thinking and value the other humans in the room.

Furniture Hacks

We love the creativity of educators. They are able to do the most with the least resources, and this definitely applies to outfitting spaces for their kids. If you're the type of person who leverages social media for hacking ideas, then you need to check out Pinterest and Twitter for furniture hacks. Educators all over the world are finding inexpensive items they can use to create different learning environments.

A lot of companies that sell flexible seating and furniture have steep price tags on their products, so finding ways to modify inexpensive furniture is a necessity for many teachers. Here are some great examples of furniture hacks:

- Use milk crates, cushions, plywood, and fabric to create seats that can be moved or stacked.
- Jennifer Hege (@jenniferbhege) used cement blocks, one-by-four planks, pillows, floor mats, lawn chairs and a couple of other inventive seating options to totally remove all desks and most tables to create an open, inviting and productive space for her sixth-grade ELA learners.
- Rich Czyz (@RACzyz) took the top of old swivel chairs and used them for floor seating.

- Nancy Brawley (@WRMS_Brawley) put her discount shopping prowess to good use to find an incredible deal on tables with casters and rolling chairs for her seventh-grade ELA room. Her room became a model for mobility, tranquility and creativity.
- Instead of painting a wall green for green screen work, buy green fabric and sew grommets on one end. Put some 3M hooks on the wall, and you have a green screen that can be assembled or disassembled quickly in the space you choose.

Friendraising: Partnering with Businesses to Help Build

 Leaders need to heed the call of Simon T. Bailey and his method for building connections in your community. At the National Principals Conference in 2017, Simon gave a passionate call for schools to stop fundraising. His idea, which is based on his research of school leaders, is called friendraising. Friendraising is about connecting our classrooms and schools to the community. It is about building relationships. As Simon said during his message, "Relationships are the currency of the future."

REVOLUTION@ARY IDEA

"You don't need money. You need a relationship."
—Simon T. Bailey

I can tell you from experience that the time and energy it takes to speak with businesses does pay off. Yes, there are some that will close the door on your idea, but if you're persistent, you can find businesses to partner with you. At South MS we have embarked on building our own furniture to fit learning spaces and the needs of our learners. Through an elevator pitch to business leaders, I vision cast the idea, and many of the business owners donated or provided material at a reduced cost.

How does this look practically? The first thing you need to do is develop a plan to pitch your idea to potential business partners. Include research, pictures of other creative learning spaces, and the reason(s) for the changes you want to make. Explain the "why" and "how" for the project by making it clear in your presentation. You know your stakeholders, so find parents associated with the business you are targeting. Then allow business partners to attach their logo and signage to the space if your central office allows it. I recommend including and allowing the businesses into the school space as much as you can. Make it a collaborative effort in the learning process.

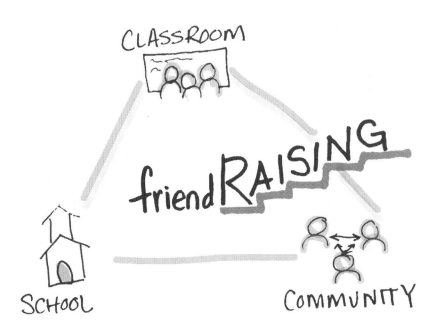

Build It as a Community

How about you take this furniture idea to a different level by including your parents? I (Darren) have discovered that I cannot afford to purchase catalog furniture, and much of it does not meet the requirements set by our learners. This isn't just an idea from my head or a group of adults. The ideas for creating the building blueprints come from the input we receive from kids, our learners. It makes no sense to have adults make all the decisions on a space that is meant for and used mostly by our kids, so I include our kids by asking what they would want or surveying them after they use the space or furniture.

After including input from learners, however, I rely on parents and their expertise to build furniture for our building. I have two types of parents who help with our furniture builds. The first type includes my highly-skilled parents who are contractors, construction workers, or just plain handy. The second type are the parents who just want to help in some way. I have discovered that lots of parents have the ability to hammer, paint, sand, clean, lift, and do much more than you ever imagined. Send a simple email to all your parents explaining your need, and you will have your own Field of Dreams. All you need to do is build relationships, ask questions, and promote a vision. It is not a matter of creativity alone; it is the ability to sell a vision.

My construction skills are limited, so I begin with a small group of skilled parents who are able to work with my rough design for flexible furniture. As they build the prototype, I take pictures and record the process. I mark the dimensions, cuts, and sizes on a sheet of paper or my iPad.

When the prototype is completed, I rely on the second group of parents. I make sure we have a skilled contractor or two on site, but it's mostly average moms and dads who simply want to help. We hold "building parties" on Saturday mornings with up to ten parents helping at different skill levels. You can watch a time-lapse video of our group building the coffeehouse-style tables (bit.ly/2QOo7jq) we use in our hallways by going to my YouTube channel (Darren Ellwein). Not only are parents using their skills to build furniture, they are also partnering with us to build school culture. Their hands are creating learning opportunities. Parents like these have the power to revolutionize a school.

REVOLUTION@ARY IDEA

Not only are parents using their skills to build furniture, but they are also now partnering with us to build school culture.
—@dellwein

But before any of that gets started, remember to ask your students how they would like to see their learning spaces used. Their thoughts and ideas can lead to uses we would never think of. Kids are the users. Include them.

Guide to including parents in your own furniture build:

1. Get input from learners and ideas from other schools.
2. Friendraise with local businesses and parents with connections.
3. Gather supplies.
4. Find two to four contractor parents who understand the vision and prototype.
5. Email all parents asking for help with mass production.
6. Include a larger group of parents to build, paint, design, sand, etc.
7. To make this time more efficient, you can pre-cut the pieces.
8. Have enough tools on site to keep the group(s) busy.

9. Survey learners to see what changes could or need to be made. (One example of this is the whiteboard tables we use in our hallways and classrooms. They are a bear to move because of their weight. Future tables will have casters on one end to roll them from place to place.)
10. Repeat these steps for new designs.

The final point I want to make is this: You *can* do this. Parents are looking for ways to connect with their children's schools, and this is one way they can literally build a culture that truly serves students. We often hear middle school and high school parents say they don't have many opportunities to serve. Here's one! Make it happen! It simply takes preparation and the right helpers.

The coffeehouse-style tables have been such a hit that we have not yet moved on to the other furniture builds. At this time we have five more furniture prototypes to produce, and I (Darren) will need to find new parents to prototype them at HSMS. Keep your ear to the ground to find the right parents for building.

REVOLUTION@ARY ACTION

Design compelling workspaces to help students do compelling work.

This age group is characterized by being energetic and needing movement. Revolutionizing spaces is the first step in personalizing learning for students. None of us learn the same way, so help kids by creating spaces that allow them options for their learning.

CALL TO ACTION

▶ What space designs in your school or classroom can you give to students?

▶ How will you capture input from students on what they want in their space?

▶ What thinking will you have to deprogram or instill to facilitate this change?

▶ What would students in your class/ school say about their workspace?

▶ What spaces in your school are underutilized? How can they be transformed?

CHAPTER 4

REVOLUTION@RY CULTURES

WE'VE ALL SEEN THOSE visuals that depict school culture as a massive iceberg floating in the ocean. The tip of the iceberg represents the small portion of school culture that's visible to the general public. The gigantic piece that remains underwater and out of sight is the true foundation of your school's culture. The hard work necessary to create an inclusive, productive, and creative school culture happens under the water.

Revolution@ries know the importance of a healthy school culture. No significant changes, learner-centered or teacher-centered, will happen if that's not in place. As revolution@ries it's our job to help build the healthy culture we want to see. It's an enormous job, but true revolution@ries know that fear will only stall a school's progress. True revolution@ries roll up their sleeves, get honest about their schools' strengths and weaknesses, and tackle the difficult conversations.

When the question of teacher-centered vs. learner-centered comes up, the revolution@ry steps up to put learners first.

A healthy culture helped us at Spring Lake Middle School, an urban, high-needs middle school near Fayetteville, North Carolina, as we endeavored to change our learning and teaching practices and to really dive into using more technology to help with student engagement and learning in the classroom. A healthy culture helps West Rowan Middle School embrace collaborative learning spaces for students outside the classroom. These are intentional shifts away from what is tried and traditional. While they challenge decades-old sentiment about learning and teaching, good vision, support, and open dialogues have helped move these initiatives along.

Revolution@ry Insight

While we can talk at length about all that a healthy school culture involves, for the sake of starting your revolution, we are going to narrow our scope. There are educators and practitioners who are more versed in school culture and have more insight into school culture than we do. As we have talked about the environments in our middle schools over this year of planning and collaborating, we have found that certain types of cultures in our schools have helped us realize certain shifts and successes in our schools. Building and developing culture is ongoing work, and no one ever reaches the top of the mountain, but part of having a healthy culture is being on board for the journey.

Instead of focusing on the entire iceberg, we are going to look at the biggest chunks of the iceberg that helped us see movement in the areas of:

- Empowerment
- Collaboration
- Student-Centered Learning
- Risk-Taking/Experimentation

Create a Culture of Empowerment

Empowerment is a critical need in schools today. As we move away from the factory model of education, we must also develop a clear vision of where we are going, what we want our student learning environments to look like, and what we want our students to be able to accomplish. As we initiate more conversations about these areas, it becomes easier to shift expectations and, eventually, practices and behavior. I (Derek) found this to be the case at WRMS. The staff at WRMS committed to this shift early by cementing it in our mission statement: Empowering students to achieve academic and personal success. Today, years after we crafted that first mission statement, it is still visible in our PBLs, our Compassion Project, and in other learner-centered work.

When we made empowerment our mission at West Rowan, we had many conversations about how to help our students be more independent. It spurred a lot of conversations and questions about our abilities as educators and how much we trust our middle schoolers:

- Do we allow these eleven-to-thirteen-year-olds to have partial independence or total independence?
- Can they handle it?
- What does independence look like in a classroom or the media center or another setting?

- How do we know if it's working?
- How do we measure success or progress in this area?

The answers to those questions did not come to us immediately. Answering them took time, patience, creativity, and a shared commitment. Because empowerment was becoming a part of what we wanted to be, it became a regular focus of our PD. PD is how we support teachers with shifting beliefs and skills. Our PD and faculty meetings shifted from sit-and-tells to active learning sessions where we modeled independent learning and creation with staff. We took time to develop our activities to the level of work we wanted to see in our classes. Eventually we started seeing a shift to less content introduction and more initial research and discovery. We started seeing teachers move from giving answers and modeling to facilitating more productive struggle.

But the shift was uncomfortable, and one persistent worry among teachers was the sheer newness of giving their students more freedom. We've never done this before—is that OK? This is a step in the journey towards empowering teachers. When there is a shift from control to release, there will be a point where learners and teachers look back to the control system for validation or approval that what they're doing is okay. This is where the shift to coach becomes necessary. We do this largely by making sure people know we are building a safe, risk-averse learning environment for everyone. A popular workout facility has a motto of being a judgement-free zone. We have to promote our schools as risk-free and judgment-free zones that continually celebrate attempts as well as solid successes.

I was a K–12 student in an era when compliance was the gold standard. It made sense to implement a factory model of education. At the time, the most common jobs demanded compliance and routine, and let's face it, a compliant, routines-based classroom is quiet and efficient. Compliance guarantees an element of order and control for the traditional educator. To be clear, Darren and I agree that schools and classrooms must have students that follow agreed-upon norms, especially when we expect high levels of empowerment and independent work. But there is a difference between compliance and buy-in, enforcing rules and building culture, conversations vs. consequences.

Compliance can't be the highest expectation.

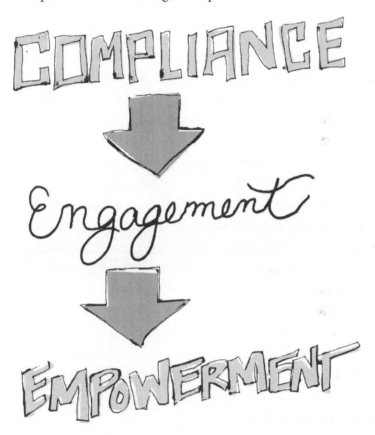

HSMS Impacting the World of Plastics

At HSMS, students are challenged to work together and create their own path to changing the world with great results. We've specifically focused on reducing plastic pollution in our waters.

It's likely something at your school needs to shift or dramatically change in order to a create a learner-centered environment.

With your Revolution@ry partner, take some time to have a conversation about what that can be:

- Rethinking collaborative spaces for students to do great work
- Making real global connections for authentic learning and exploration
- Creating different opportunities for students to give input and have a voice
- Making real efforts to trust 11-, 12-, and 13-year-olds in your building by using adult language, rules, and action
- Rethinking learning and demonstration expectations so that all students have an opportunity to be successful

There are many great books out there, particularly in the Pirate Library, that can help you transform your school culture to be more responsive to the needs of students. We aren't going to focus on the hows, but we do encourage you to do so. We are going to dive deep into some indicators and how they help us empower and get the most out of our learners.

The key to making the changes we are sharing in this book is the make-or-break factor that enables/empowers the change in beliefs and practices in any school: shifting the culture.

Revolution@ry Mindset

At WRMS, by loosening the reins a bit, we moved a step beyond compliance into engagement. Student engagement is necessary for authentic learning, and while you want your middle schoolers to be excited and involved and invested, you can't stop there. Compliance doesn't fuel a desire for life long learning, it simply reinforces a desire to play the game of school to get by and get out. Engaged learners can develop an appreciation of continuing their education because they find value in their learning experiences. Empowered learners know they have control and realize that their values and passions play a part in their learning. They are likely to continue to take risks, try new things, and have a healthy perspective on failure and risk. A school must give its students the power—everything from permission and tools to time and creative freedom—to stimulate and navigate their own learning. True learning happens when we create moments for learners to struggle and create their own solutions. Sometimes it's as simple as students and teachers working side by side, planning and agreeing on how a topic will be explored. Other times it might be as simple—or revolution@ry—as a teacher asking a student, "What do you want to learn?" and "Why do you want to learn that?" and then allowing it to happen.

Nancy Brawley (@wrmsreads) was a seventh-grade ELA teacher for many years. She took our talks and PD to heart and cleverly began to rethink how seventh-grade ELA standards can and should be taught. She created a problem-based challenge for all her classes, including all levels of learners: a marketing campaign for our school. Over the years our school had been struggling with some community image issues: waning achievement scores, a disconnect between community and school, a misperception of unruliness in our hallways. No matter how hard we worked, it was a persistent struggle to improve our image.

Mrs. Brawley focused on two inspirations: 1) Turning this concern into a PBL, and 2) Giving students real empowerment to experiment and create. Instead of setting tight parameters, she focused on meeting a need for the school and touched on the heartstrings of her seventh graders. I spent days in her classroom in the weeks to follow, and I heard students debating different areas to explore, sharing with others why their "why" changed and how the products they chose would best fit and represent the needs they were addressing. We get the best opportunities for learning and empowerment when we provide a trusting, caring environment for our learners to work in. The learning outcomes started with the standards in mind, but we were focused on providing learners with skills they would need in a further stage in life. In the end we saw as many varied thoughts as you can imagine, from videos we displayed on social media to posters and flyers we distributed. It's also important to note that the end products weren't the only ways the standard was measured. There were also several benchmarks students had to reach along the way. The payoff in demonstrated learning and high-interest investment can't be measured.

Let's spend some time on the following activity. We want you to think of what compliance, engagement, and empowerment mean to you. In the allotted space, jot some thoughts about what each would look like in the areas listed on the left. Record all your thoughts, no matter how general or specific. We've listed two subjects (Math and Social Studies), but you can write this for any subject area.

	Compliance	Engagement	Empowerment
Teacher Activity			
Learner Activity			
Math Class			
Social Studies Class			
Professional Learning			
Lesson Planning			

When we place a high value on empowerment, our learners, teachers, and colleagues develop the confidence to try to be creative.

Teachers who empower students spark passions in their students that can take them to amazing places in life. Empowered students go on to question the status quo, think creatively and critically, solve impossible problems, and serve the greater good. At revolution@ry middle schools, teachers aren't simply preparing learners for high school—they're preparing them for the rest of their lives. The checklist mentality of compliance provides comfort, but empowerment makes us ready for life.

Create a Culture of Collaboration

We live in a world where problems are becoming more complex: economic crises, digital divides, battles over open access to information, and environmental catastrophes. The reality is that many of these problems will likely be solved in the near future by the learners in our classrooms. What's even more likely is that they will do it in collaboration with another person or a team of people. Our world is more connected—digitally, socially, economically—than ever before, and learning and problem-solving must become more collaborative.

We must commit to shifting our delivery and design from task-orientation (simple problem/simple solution) to creative, collaborative exploration and solution design. While we might have always wanted students to be problem solvers in our schools, the scope of the problems-and-solutions generation might have been limited. Reflect back on some of the old school textbooks you used in the classroom. At the end of each chapter, there were the standard wrap-up questions most teachers would assign their students to answer. Below those questions were often some tougher questions with a title like "Problem

Solving" to serve as a more advanced challenge. Many teachers—and I (Derek) was guilty of this too—gave these questions little consideration. Teaching with mediocre expectations has become a common phenomenon in education, and although I assigned interesting projects occasionally and made extra credit available to everyone, complex problem-solving and collaboration weren't the norm.

REVOLUTION@ARY REFLECTION

Are our school/classroom practices preparing students for a world that values collaboration and teamwork?

Many of us have been taught to believe that only some of our students are capable of working out these more complex problems independently, which is a misguided notion. As a result, those students and the more rigorous work have been set apart into unique classes. (This isn't just a middle school practice that must be revolutionized—it's our entire approach to learning!)

In a recent *Inc.* article, Richard Branson, founder of Virgin Group, said that collaboration is the ultimate key to success. He shared how leadership models have evolved from the lonely figure at the top of the mountain to the energetic and collaborative team player. "To be successful in business, and in life, you need to connect and collaborate," Branson said. He went on to share ten of his favorite quotes about collaboration and success, and the list of thinkers who inspire him includes everyone from Louisa May Alcott ("It takes two flints to make a fire.") to Vince Lombardi ("Individual commitment to a group effort—that is what makes a team work, a company work, a society work, a civilization work."). Consider your classroom in those same terms. Do you recognize students only for earning the high marks? Or do you also recognize those who work together to make progress? [Richard Branson's 10 Favorite Quotes on Collaboration https://buff.ly/2QiQBXx]

There is a real need to redesign the work and environments in our schools to make them purposeful and worthwhile. We should take time to ensure that what we design or agree upon for our schools taps into the social aspect of learning. As educators we sometimes deliberately confuse learning with completion or checking boxes or filling in blanks. We often confuse completion of an activity with what we want students to learn, and they are not the same. The same can be said of teachers in collaborative planning teams. We are taught to develop norms and understandings for working together professionally so we can create worthwhile learning experiences for all students in our learning spaces, no matter what their level of understanding. The best planning comes from taking the time to explore, having conversations (or debates if we have to) about what is best, and then making it happen. This applies to both learners and teachers in our schools. Rushing through to completion focuses on the task, but collaboration helps us focus on the learning we do along the way.

REVOLUTION@ARY IDEA

Revolution@ries must do their part to make collaborative learning the norm.

What does a culture of collaboration look like? Throughout the years, Darren and I have invested in the following areas to create more collaborative teams at our schools:

- Creating inviting spaces for students and staff to create in

- Creating norms for working in these spaces
- Designing projects that stir up excitement
- Creating flexibility in how learning is demonstrated
- Coaching learners to consider different perspectives and drive towards results
- Setting high expectations

Staff from WRMS visited Meadow Glenn Middle in South Carolina. This school, under the leadership of Dr. Bill Coon, is the only Expeditionary Learning middle school in South Carolina. For nine years, they have been doing great things with student-led learning and deep dive, and it took them years to build that culture of learning. Our goal was not to replicate everything we saw from Meadow Glenn and create a clone in North Carolina, but we did have a desire to bring some of the features back that helped facilitate their culture of collaboration. We focused on two particular concepts: norms for collaboration (for teachers and learners) and habits of learning, which we eventually adopted as our core values.

We realized that creating working norms for learners and teachers must be at the forefront. If we wanted to see real, high-quality work, we had to establish concrete guidelines. Everyone had to be taught—or at least reminded—how to work together. Everyone.

Norms aren't new. Developing norms for PLCs has been essential for many years. When we brought these norms back to WRMS, we talked about what had to happen in order for the best to be developed. We called these norms "Our Understandings":

- Weigh in, then buy in
- Assume the best intent
- Be present and respectful
- Disagreement and confusion must be communicated
- Have a bias towards yes

This shift to a collaborative culture must be the work of the collective. We had to teach everyone in our schools—learners, teachers, and parents—how to plan, work, and create together. Even though real learning is a social exercise, we haven't always done a great job of teaching the social aspect of working together. We have to take time to develop, share, and teach so that the best ideas are created and shared. We don't engage in high-level planning simply to better ourselves: we commit to high-level planning so our learners can win! We began talking about these expectations in our content planning, during teacher PD sessions, at leadership meetings, and at as many group gatherings as possible.

Making collaboration one of our core values was difficult but worthwhile work. It wasn't just about being able to sit across from a person you know or like and have easy conversations. It was about sharing ideas and setting goals, both face-to-face and virtually. It was about valuing diverse voices and backgrounds to work towards a common cause. We began to use collaboration to frame all our day-to-day work and our special projects at WRMS. It was a key foundation for our Compassion Project.

A meaningful lesson on collaborating with my admin group came in the summertime during some PD sessions with the North Carolina PD group DRIVE. Our coach, Charlie, led us through building a house of cards as high as we could and as quickly as we could. I offered a suggestion for how to build it, and it sounded good—why wouldn't it?—and we went with it. After we built the house, we had a reflection period. As we talked about the experience, I remembered that I often overlook an important fact about myself that I continually have to manage—valuing suggestions more than the process. This led to a good reminder about Our Understandings and the need we have for them. Our Understandings create a safe space for us to share suggestions with people, and in order for us to value the process, we have to value those suggestions.

We have to teach the expectation to realize the greatness!

In our experience, whenever collaboration happened, we were able to ask more of our students. Learning experiences became more meaningful, and students placed a greater value on the contributions of their classmates. We created opportunities for self-directed learning!

I saw this reinforced during one of my visits to Darren's school. Two learners scheduled a time to present a community project to him that would help with an initiative to reduce the use of plastics in local restaurants. On their own, they saw how this could happen and developed a plan to make it a reality.

Collaboration isn't the polite, surface-level talk we once used to associate quiet classrooms with good classrooms. It's complex work and real progress. The Revolution@ry's role is to check, monitor, push, and hold expectations to a high level.

Create a Culture of Student-Centered Learning

One of the most powerful gifts and contributions we can make to our field is relinquishing our outdated perceptions of control. When we got together for this book and brainstormed what we wanted to see happen in middle schools, one of the first things we discussed was what the classroom would look like, specifically in contrast to how we were taught to treat/manage middle school learners. Classroom management has been about management and authority. We had to have that level of dominance over hormonal students since they were, after all, out of control.

One indication that this type of thinking is consistent across our field is that you'll often hear educators say they don't mind "noise in their classroom" or that you are "likely to see a lot of chaos" going on if you visit their room. You will often hear this from a revolution@ry who is trying to make sure people nearby know that learning is a priority, even though they see a need to do it differently. This talk bothers us because we shouldn't have to make an excuse to explain what best learning practices are! Making the shift from desks in rows to flexible seating shouldn't require permission or defending. Making the needs of the different learners in our room a priority shouldn't have to be excused. We should replace "You'll likely hear noise" with "Come by my room and you'll experience learning."

Rick Wormeli is a champion of rethinking learning and teaching practices and what we do at our schools. We had a great talk with him about the need for shifting practices at the school level, particularly at the middle level. So much of what we do in the classroom is counter to how the brain of a learner works, especially the brain of a middle schooler.

Our static, centuries-old practice of grading does not fit the need of a still-forming brain that is looking for opportunities to try and retry.

1. We can't exclude emotions and feelings from what we design in our learning environments. When we set up classroom rules or expectations and enforce classroom management, we are often doing so to limit the expression of feelings or to limit various students. We have to make sure we are building a culture that respects and includes the voices of all who come to the table. Students can't leave feelings and emotions at the door. They are as much a part of the learning process as the content we design and deliver.

2. Inflexibility kills learning. It kills enthusiasm and creativity. Inflexible grading policies don't allow students to try and retry as needed. Think of a time when an inflexible practice prohibited you from trying again when you knew you would have gotten it right the second (or fourth) time. Grading is in desperate need of a revolution. Often it has nothing to do with

learning. Inflexibility in class design also stifles learning. P. Dan Wiwchar is attributed as saying, "Your brain can absorb only what your ass can endure." The more we sit, the less we are engaged. We think he wrote this just for us (wishful thinking).

Take some time to watch Rick's insightful thirty-minute interview

When we talk about learner-centered practices or what happens during the learner-centered shift, we go into detail about three other major areas we have focused on in our schools on our journey to create learner-centered environments. When we speak on the importance of flexibility, we share how we allow students to demonstrate their learning or understanding of essential standards/content. It can't just be about giving a multiple-choice test where we're looking for a specific number to tell us that learning happened. It's powerful to give students a choice in what to explore, how to explore it, or, in this case, how they demonstrate learning. Digital tools like Popplet, Flipgrid, and movie creation apps let students get creative with their demonstration and explanation of what they learned.

This leads to another practice: embracing technology. Technology is a gap closer: achievement, experience, confidence, relationship, etc. It is a powerful accelerator for the committed revolution@ry who makes learning more about web searching low-level topics or typing papers. Technology can connect learners to the world. It gives a voice to introverts. It is a tool learners can use to astonish us if we allow it.

The third element we emphasize for creating a learner-centered culture is the evolved role of the educator in the learning environment.

We want to see educators move from the old role of director and instructor to that of a relationship builder and content designer. We want educators who are not afraid to push their own limits and the limits of the learners in the room to do whatever is needed and not just what is most convenient. This is hard work because we are all hard wired from our own experience to be that director or instructor, but learners don't need that. The world doesn't need that.

We need revolution@ries.

We developed these guiding questions to help you in your journey towards creating a learner-centered culture:

- Where do students go to refocus their thoughts?
- Where do students/teachers go to re-engage their thinking?
- What can learners/teachers do to reinvigorate creative thinking?
- How can learners celebrate one another's accomplishments?
- What does choice look like in class? The library? The lunchroom? Before/after school?

Create a Culture of Risk-Taking

We don't want anyone, learners or teachers, to lose hope when they try new things and don't get the results they expect or want. In our world of highly-complex problems, we must resolve to continue working for solutions until we see results. The all-or-nothing mindset is one of the major faults of our old system of thinking. That kind of thinking only encourages learners to look for the areas they're "good at" instead of learning to consistently chip away at a problem until solving it.

We all know the old adage, "If at first you don't succeed, try, try again." If we truly believed this as a society, we would do a lot of things differently in education. We would grade differently (we wouldn't put topics on a timetable) and we would stop comparing students by their rankings and their grades.

Our focus on getting specific results and looking for specific outcomes makes it really easy for us to look for safe, tried-and-true methods. When we make the end result the goal, not the process or the attempts, we look for what's safe and often what's easy. We see this every day in the classroom—what program will increase our Lexile scores? What planning process will yield higher achievement results? Which method teaches the math steps better? All of these are questions I asked during my career until someone challenged me with a better question—what do your learners need?

Mellotta Hill, the 2015 Principal of the Year for Cumberland County Schools in North Carolina, shared a piece of advice with me that puts risk-taking practices into perspective: there are very few tough decisions, but there are often tough conversations. Do you know the changes that need to be made to your classroom or grade level that will bring about more learner-centered action? If so, are you willing to have tough conversations with your principal to see them implemented? If you are a lead learner at a school, are you willing to have that conversation with a teacher/teammate who might not get it? Now ask yourself if you are the reason that conversation might be difficult.

We have to make risk less risky. We have to create safe spaces for challenging discussions to take place, especially if they challenge what we fundamentally believe or have been doing for years.

- **Stay Human:** Acknowledge feelings of fear and trepidation. It might take time for some people to bring their risky thoughts forward.

- **Redefine Failure:** When you don't get the results you wanted, use your "failure" as an opportunity to recalibrate and move forward.

REVOLUTION@ARY IDEA

Redefine failure as learning.

- **Provide Opportunity for Struggle:** Encourage everyone around you to get off the sidelines and become a part of the process.
- **Help Learning Happen:** Remove hurdles by limiting feedback to what will spur growth and consideration while avoiding value judgments.

CALL TO ACTION

▶ What would your (middle) school look like if you embraced one of these subcultures?

▶ What would your journey look like?

▶ How would learner participation change?

▶ How would adult practice change?

CHAPTER 5

REVOLUTION@RY CONNECTIONS

DRONES! I (**DARREN**) **LOVE** working with drones. The only thing better than working with them personally is seeing kids' eyes light up when they can drive or fly one themselves. Drones have been integral in the work that HSMS has done with schools globally.

It was May 2015, and our building was going to have a Teach Like a Pirate (TLAP) Day, a chance for students to select their learning based on teacher passions. I planned to lead a drone experience and took a picture of a student flying a drone before school began that day. In the tweet, I tagged #drones, which got a response from Terje Pedersen (@terjepe) in Norway. He responded by sending an engaging video of his students working with different types of technology, including drones.

I had a feeling this was a school with a similar mindset to ours, a school that could do some serious "damage" educationally. I didn't know Terje and was admittedly nervous about this connection. We had a video chat that same day and agreed to talk again in August. That simple photo on Twitter has created multiple opportunities for learning despite our schools being seven hours (and an ocean) apart.

Networking with Norway

When August rolled around the following school year, I messaged Terje via Twitter. I was hopeful that this connection would have more depth to it because too many educators stop at only cultural exchanges. I wanted to transform learning and quickly discovered that Terje shared that goal. We forged an amazing relationship that has brought our students together via video chats to hold forums, edit artifacts, and more. We collaborated on a plan to connect teachers, students, and relevant topics in our curricula. Terje is a revolution@ry! In what way? If he is going to study discrimination against Native Americans, he finds first-person accounts and connects them to his students. If his students are studying about Apartheid, he locates the people who experienced it. We both were driven to produce authentic learning outcomes. This shared passion helped things really take off.

During that first year, our students collaborated on four projects within five months. Where did we start? The first resource we needed was interested teachers. We started with English-language arts (ELA). First, we wanted our students to critique one another's writing. We did this using Google Apps, specifically Google Docs, but then added a personal piece to allow them to connect beyond the screen: video chats. The problem? A seven-hour time difference. It was the first test of persistence. We were determined to find a solution so our students could engage with one another in video chats.

After some thought, Terje shared an idea. He had his Norwegian students lengthen their school day so that it aligned with the start of our day in central daylight time. Instead of arriving at school at the normal time in Bergen, Norway, they arrived one hour later, thereby lengthening their school day. In South Dakota, the timing paired perfectly with an ELA class that began first period. As a result of that creative fix, our learners were able to connect in real time and discuss content and topics.

The connections were a set of video chats. At first, we used Google Hangouts, but we later switched to Appear.in to facilitate these discussions because it provided streamlined access to the discussion. After we had the initial get-to-know-you out of the way, the learning was off and running at top speed.

Mentoring in English

Pedersen wanted our students to mentor Bergen students in their use of the English language. Using Appear.in, the students critiqued spoken and written language components. Students were placed in groups of two or three and had a peer group across the ocean. It was common to have ten or more video chat groups working at the same time during a collaborative session. Appear.in made it easy because it only requires a link to join.

It didn't stop there. Together, we also explored Native American issues. Because South Dakota has several Native American reservations, this was a great fit for our students and relevant to our state history. We created a private Facebook group for our students to discuss topics like culture, prejudices, and stereotypes. This effort went further than we could have expected. The kids used Google to search for experts who could participate in our discussions. They found two Native Americans who work with the U.S. Department of Justice in South Dakota. Those officials came to our school to visit with our learners, and we connected them via video to the students in Bergen, Norway.

This endeavor expanded to include another of the ELA classes in our building. The topic resonated so much with another of my teachers that she wanted her students to connect with Terje's classroom in Norway as well. HSMS learners arrived early to school, and we implemented a Padlet discussion board on the same topic. Padlet provided a medium for real-time discussion and questioning. The conversation also included a group of Native American students who provided live input on the topics we were discussing.

This experience was only possible because there were teachers willing to choose a different approach to learning on the topic. These teachers and kids were willing to take the risk and connect globally. They could see the value in creating an experience that would provide deeper learning.

Risk = Reward

We see three levels of learning that happen on a global scale. We believe the greatest benefit to our kids comes from participating in global empathy projects, but you need a strong partner or partners to make it a reality. Global empathy is thinking with a global perspective in the learning process. It focuses on information or cues that might not be discovered unless you are learning with someone from another culture.

Our kids learn perspectives on a global scale by connecting with people outside the United States. They could always pick up a book or go online, but nothing compares to interacting with educators and students from other countries. The world is shrinking more quickly than you want to believe. With the advancement of tech tools, it has never been easier to connect with educators and students around the world. Making these connections takes time, energy, and a growth mindset. When you do it effectively, the results are revolution@ry!

Three Levels of Global Learning

As I have collaborated with my Norwegian colleagues, I have begun to view learning with schools globally in three forms: Cultural Exchange, Authentic Learning, and Global Empathy.

1. Cultural Exchange: I believe this is where most educators begin and, unfortunately, where most of them stay. Connecting with a teacher or school from another country has become easier, and the best way to begin is by getting to know one another's cultures and norms. This is the easy part. It is the introduction and questioning stage. Why do most people stay in this stage? One, I believe it is hard to maintain a connection with the pressure of a rolling curriculum. This is certainly true for us in the United States. Do me a favor and throw the formalities of the scope and sequence out the window! Think creatively about how you can cover standards. Second, differing school calendars, schedules, and time zones create a wedge in our connections. For example, schools in Europe plan several week-long holidays during the school year, whereas schools in the United States do not.

2. Authentic Learning: This level involves planning actual lessons together with a goal of fitting the standards into the learning. Too often we make the mistake of fitting the learning into the standards. Shift your thinking on this for the sake of our kids! Just let the learning be organic and discover ways to bring standards into the equation. Learning is about discovery and asking questions, not forcing a standard lesson down their throats. In my experience this requires two key components: consistency and persistence. Because schedules, time zones, and holidays can disrupt the relationship, you have to commit to making this happen. You need to be consistent in maintaining the connections and ideas. You have to value and practice persistence when the date of an activity is moved back three or four times due to various issues. If you can weather these issues, the rewards are fabulous! Here are some examples...

English Mentors—Most countries require English as a second language. This requirement fits in well with the editing and refining of written and verbal work.

Math Problem Solving—Kim Aarberg is another growth mindset educator from Norway. He teaches on the island of Askoy, just outside Bergen, and has collaborated with our learners on various math projects. Math is one of the more difficult subjects to tag with creativity, but we used Flipgrid as the medium to learn about the area of different shapes. The goal was to solve a math problem provided by a group of learners from Norway. Flipgrid allowed us to use video to see the problem and respond to it. The response had to detail the pathway we used to solve the problem. When all these different paths were collected on Flipgrid, the learners could see variations in thinking that all led to the same answer.

Drones and the Pythagorean Theorem—One of Terje Pedersen's colleagues, Anne-Marit Selstø, had been using drones to learn coordinate planes. Expanding on this idea, we created a lesson that used our Parrot Jumping Sumo drones to explain the Pythagorean theorem. We also used Parrot's quadcopter and Sphero robots to teach about coordinate planes. These activities were shared between our schools, and teachers also set up challenges on selected Fridays during the year.

Snapchat and History—Another project we did with the Rothaugen Skole in Bergen involved Snapchat. Snapchat has plenty of negative press, especially when you're talking about middle school students, but it offers learning possibilities as well. Snapchat has a lot of filter options, and we decided to create a lesson using the face swap feature. To bring the French Revolution alive, learners had to create a Snap mashing their face with a person from the French Revolution and write a dialogue to fit the historical context. The Snaps were then shared between the two groups.

The Benefits of Global Connection
by Revolution@ry Educator
Kim Nilsen Aarberg (@KAarberg)

The Norwegian school-system relies on pedagogical freedom and trust from our leaders. As luck will have it, my assistant principal trusted me so that I can make the decision for my students on how I want to give them an authentic experience in their learning process. That being said, not all schools in Norway are the same, and this varies to some extent across the country, as I believe it does in most European countries. Given this amount of freedom comes with a cost. It took me several years before I found other teachers to work with, who shared my view on how education was supposed to look like. My biggest source of influence came from Terje Pedersen in Bergen, Norway. He has always pushed me forward and has a similar teaching style as me.

In our teaching, we try to connect with other teachers, leaders and even experts around the world for more inspiration. At one point I came across Darren Ellwein, and as luck would have it, he also shared the same thoughts as us. He has also introduced us to other peers around the States so that we can do more projects together. Through our collaboration we have connected with so many inspiring people, both teachers and students. Our projects continue to grow and develop at its own pace. One of the main issues was how to tackle the time zone difference, seven hours to be exact. This is where our system has a great benefit, and again I'm thinking about the trust we are given by leaders and parents. We have good communication with the homes of every student, and we can have students stay at school longer than a normal school day. On some occasions the students came back to the classroom three or four hours after the school day has ended. When you see your entire class come back to do a Q&A with another group of students across the Atlantic Ocean, it makes you proud and hopeful for this generation of learners.

It also tells me that our kids really want to learn at school. The big impact, and this is my own view and not relied on science, has to be the authentic learning experience. When you combine this with communication and collaboration with others, the magic happens.

The Norwegian school system is far from perfect, but we are given trust in our approach on methods to use in our classroom. A teacher in a global classroom is never alone, and the effort in creating a global classroom benefits students in my classroom and classrooms across oceans. Now, advancements in technology make authentic learning a reality. This collaboration just keeps on growing and the classroom gets bigger each year we are doing this.

3. Global Empathy: I explained this to some extent already, but global empathy hinges on something this generation possess in high quantities: empathy. We have seen that if you can attract the emotions and heart of a learner, they will passionately learn. As a matter of fact, they probably won't even know they are learning because they are "All In." How do you draw out global empathy in your learners? By connecting the learning to a real problem or cause.

Native Peoples—Earlier in this chapter, I talked about a Native American project we studied with students in Norway. Every country has an aboriginal population, and I wanted our kids in Harrisburg to understand a global thread. When we worked with Terje in Bergen, Norway, we learned about the Sami people who were in northern parts of Norway. Learning about Native American and Sami people allowed us to find parallels and differences between these two groups.

Writing on the Wall—Sven Olaf Brekke of Odda, Norway, was gracious enough to include our eighth graders in a project called The Writing on the Wall. Sven is the headmaster, or principal, of his school and has become another dear friend in our effort to change education for the better. In the fall of each year, his students write a short text based on a prompt. In 2017, we worked with him to discuss the topic of "Capital," as in human capital, opening our learners' minds to the diversity in this topic. Here is more about Sven's Writing on the Wall.

THE WRITING ON THE WALL
BY REVOLUTION@RY EDUCATOR
SVEN OLAF BREKKE (@SVENOLAFBREKKE)

"The Writing on the Wall" is a collaborative text-project started at Odda secondary school in Norway. The project began as a wish to include students in a national literature symposium hosted in the city of Odda each October. The symposium has a new theme every year. Earlier themes have been Home, Trouble, Help, Capital, and so forth. The symposium has been going on for seventeen years.

Odda secondary school has worked particularly on writing short texts, sometimes called "Twitter-texts." By introducing the theme to the students, collaborating upon what to associate with the theme, the students have come up with a lot of very fine texts. Each text is written on a Google slide. In this way, all the contributors can see everyone's texts. We have also done artwork connected to the theme and placed pictures of these in between the text-slides in the Google presentation. You can see one of the presentations going in a loop on this link: goo.gl/R9zaSV.

The final presentation is projected on a wall at the centre of Odda, thereby earning the name, "writing on the wall." The writing on the wall is a biblical saying, predicting an omen. Today, with Facebook, "writing on the wall" has a different meaning.

Next year we want to introduce historical photographs from our area of Norway and try to let them be an inspiration to texts along with the theme. We always invite other schools (from Norway and other countries) to join the project.

Developing Ideas

The "How?" question is probably still on the fringe of most minds right now. How do we get to this place of learning in these projects? For us it begins with direct messages on Twitter that look like these examples:

- "Do you have any connections with the juvenile justice system in the United States? I want to develop a project comparing and contrasting the juvenile justice systems in our countries."
- "Let's get ahold of the author of this book to walk with our learners through this unit. It will tie into the objective for this project."
- "I have an idea to take water samples to test microplastics. Know any scientists who can help?"

Notice that these ideas did not start with "I have a standard that needs to be addressed..." or "I need to hit the standard _____ this month..." Too many times the focus is on a standard and not on the world in which our kids are living. It's no wonder our learners become disinterested in learning at school. We need to stop forcing standards, and policies related to a timeline standards should be taught, throwing them down the throats of our learners. Doing so creates a sterile environment for learning.

The difference in the pursuit of authentic learning and global empathy with our colleagues in Norway revolves around real, relevant events. If you go to Terje's blog (rothaugenglobalclassroom.blogspot.com), he has real examples of his students connecting with people around the world. These connections result in learning outcomes and memorable learning experiences. Isn't this what learning is about? His blog includes practical learning ideas instead of worksheets on a topic.

How Far Can This Go?

It may not be possible for everyone, but we had several middle school kids travel to other countries in the summers of 2017 and 2018. Be persistent in your connections and build relationships. Good things will happen every time you focus on relationships. Social media has made connecting very easy, but you have to consistently connect with others to foster that collaborative spirit.

When Terje and I were doing a video call one morning, he mentioned a project with the United Nations Educational, Scientific and Cultural Organization (UNESCO) out of New Delhi, India. It was sponsored by the Mahatma Gandhi Institute of Education for Peace and Sustainable Development. UNESCO was looking to bring kids from several nations around the world to Delhi. They even said they were going to pay for two students and a teacher to fly to Delhi for a conference on certain issues. Honestly, I thought it was far-fetched, but I am always willing to check out big ideas to see how far they can go. And did this go far! There were moments when it seemed as if it would not materialize, but in the end, we had two middle school boys and one teacher, Matt Dick (@techducation), fly to Delhi, India. Matt is a great risk-taker at HSMS. The boys and Matt met with students and teachers from India, Malaysia, South Africa, and Norway to discuss the topic of human migration. One of the greatest takeaways for the boys was the diverse learning of the other cultures.

Take a second and think about that. Two boys and a teacher from South Dakota were able to fly to India solely for the purpose of educational and cultural advancement! Our kids met students from four other countries to discuss issues on the global scene, such as migration. Our kids experienced an entirely different culture and also had to manage their independence since their parents weren't along for the ride. This is learning, and it is becoming more common. How persistent are you in finding opportunities like this?

Lionfish, Bats, and Iguanas, Oh My!

I could speak passionately to you about the issue of plastic pollution in our world today. We have kids at our school who are anti-plastic pollution activists. Most people who follow this topic live near the ocean, so they are surprised when they see the work our learners in land-locked South Dakota have produced on this issue. Through our science curriculum and global connections to scientists on Twitter, our work to fight plastic pollution and bring awareness to the problem has hit the global empathy stage of learning. There are several pieces of their work in this book, and as a result of their efforts, we recently were a part of a first-time event.

I can't speak enough about connecting, which is something that happened when I attended a unique conference in 2018 called the International Marine Debris Conference in San Diego. Most people thought it was strange to have a principal attending, but they found it even more unique that I was from South Dakota, a landlocked state. The result? I don't know if I have ever learned more from any other conference I have attended. Education should be about seeing problems and solving them, and this conference was about a lot of problems and the science behind them. The most beneficial piece, though, was the number of global contacts I collected for my school. I had a stack of business cards with people willing to speak to our kids about nurdles, ghost netting, microfibers, microplastics, and more.

Our work with plastic pollution also led us to connect with EdActsGlobal, a non-profit in Southern California. Fred Ramirez, CEO of EdActs, contacted me about a trip he wanted to organize for our learners and others around the world. It would be the first of its kind, and the setting would be the MesoAmerican reef, one of the largest coral reefs in the world. He had some experience working with the locals on a bay island off the mainland of Honduras called Utila.

This was another I-have-to-see-it-to-believe-it event, but it became a reality. South Middle School sent ten kids to Utila, Honduras for an amazing experience. The learning was off the charts! During the eight-day trip, they immersed themselves in the island's ecosystems and coral reef and also got to enjoy some of the local sights. Our students were able to:

- Snorkel while collecting data on fish populations
- Study fish species
- View the dissection of lionfish, which are venomous and invasive to the reef ecosystem
- Work with Kanahau Research Center on bat caves, beach cleanups to help nesting turtles, capturing/tagging/collecting data on iguana species, and mangrove education
- Present information at a conference on plastic pollution
- Lead lessons in art and music education at a local elementary school

Because I was on this trip, I can tell you firsthand how incredible it was. The impact of the island's beauty combined with the unique learning opportunities had a revolution@ry effect on our kids. How many thirteen-year-olds can say they helped embed an ID chip into an endangered iguana and watch an intern collect blood samples to check for plastic chemicals in its body? Life-changing! Opportunities like these are all around us, but you have to grab hold of them when they appear.

School Beyond Walls

Connections should not be solely for educators. When it's possible and appropriate, they should also benefit our learners. Too often learning is a passive process. Our students can get information from books, websites, and their teachers, but I believe the best learning is lived! Giving our students these kinds of opportunities promotes a true embedding of knowledge and empathy. How do you begin such a journey? Here are a few points to consider if you are willing to revolutionize your classroom:

Set a goal: Decide if you want a cultural or curricular connection.

- **Find partners:** Facebook Groups, PenPal Schools, Twitter personal learning network (PLN). These are just a few resources to help make an initial connection. My best success has come from locating people on Twitter from other countries. Most countries have a Twitter chat where you can view profiles or see comments that fit your vision and outcome.

Choose a communication platform: Find the best avenue for sharing and communicating. Note: Think Safety. When using Facebook, private groups provide a sheltered arena for learning. Honestly, our learners cringe at using Facebook and want to delete the account when they're done because their parents use Facebook. Figures. Always make parents aware of the learning outcome and allow them to decline use of the platform if they have concerns. You will also want to follow the COPPA regulations on social media use.

- **Network capabilities:** Consult your tech department about available tools and bandwidth issues. You will need to justify the "why" of opening the network as well. This could be a battle, but you need to push to make these authentic experiences happen.
- **Recruit teachers/facilitators:** Seek out people willing to take risks, use their time, and share content.

Set clear expectations for students: Be clear regarding the goal of the project; set expectations.

- **Be persistent:** Finding the right fit for your vision and school is key. Be persistent in seeking the right collaborator to produce amazing learning.

CALL TO ACTION

▶ What do you do with this chapter?

▶ Which of the three levels of Global Learning are you at?

▶ How can you use a global connection to change the learning in your school?

We challenge you to make your own revolution@ry connections abroad. Use #revoltLAP on Twitter to share the amazing learning you are doing with someone globally.

CHAPTER 6

REVOLUTION@RY INNOVATIONS

REVOLUTION@RY CHANGE HAS ALREADY begun in our world. If you walk into a new or remodeled Panera or McDonald's, you likely will not talk to an employee until you receive your food. Kiosks have replaced people. The likelihood of children under the age of six not needing a driver's license to get from one place to another increases each day with the advancement of driverless cars.

How does this sea of change compare to K–12 education? In one sense, there's no comparison. It's 2019, and we continue to teach students within and according to a century-old factory model of education. What was needed in the late nineteenth and early twentieth centuries was a system to produce a workforce for the assembly line, to produce workers who would meet the needs of the factories of the Industrial Revolution. Schools were called upon to provide information to children. This method was considered by many to be the only way to educate a population made up primarily of farmers. To call it outdated today is an understatement. We would argue that this model of education is not only obsolete—it's also detrimental.

Our students are no longer heading into an Industrial Revolution. They are heading into the first third of the twenty-first century. They are heading into a rapidly-changing world that will require skills that even the sharpest minds among us have yet to identify. Information is at their fingertips to consume, but the world needs more than consumers of information. Today's society needs producers of ideas and innovators of future products. The Industrial Revolution needed people to act like robots, but now we need people to make robots and other innovations.

To navigate this world, our students will have to think on their feet. They will have to be agile thinkers, proficient not only in critical thinking but also in negotiation, collaboration, decision making, and people management. To make that happen, we must revolutionize the way we teach students to think. And we should begin as early as kindergarten. Let's get the insurgency started!

Here's to the Future!

Consider the graphic above. What messages are these advancements and innovations sending? What do think should go in the fourth column?

As the title of our chapter indicates, we believe in revolution@ry innovation. Innovation is change with value and purpose, not change for the sake of change. It is change that solves a problem and makes life more efficient. There is no foolproof way to predict the next innovations on the horizon, but there are ways to make innovation more likely to happen, to nurture it and help it along, so to speak. When this happens, innovation becomes the norm instead of the exception.

What are our schools doing to make innovation a reality? What type of thinking is needed to promote innovation at your school? At any school? We say an innovative school promotes flexible thinking, allows staff and students to take risks, and celebrates the process of creating. And this flexible thinking, risk-taking, and creating can happen in any subject—math, science, social studies, physical education, art or English-language arts. Our elementary, middle, and high schools are entirely capable of producing a wide array of innovators—entrepreneurs, makers, and influencers—right alongside the surgeons, welders, physicists, firemen, and accountants. All it takes is a resolve to accept and reward some new mindsets and skills.

This idea, unfortunately, is not the norm in education circles across the United States. Most educators continue to rely on a prescribed curriculum, feeding it to their students according to a one-size-fits-all schedule. We think today's students want more authenticity in their learning. They appreciate having an active voice in what they are learning. They want a chance to learn while living out their passion or solving problems that matter to them.

Creating Entrepreneurs

Don Wettrick (@DonWettrick) is a teacher in Indiana who has created a course called Innovation and Open Source Learning that has an entrepreneurial focus for high school students. Don and his book, *Pure Genius,* have been influential in our work. His maverick standard of creating an entrepreneurial mindset in young people has saved many kids from the static educational structure that often turns learners into mere students. Don focuses his energy on high school learners and their projects that solve the problems they notice in our world.

If you're wondering why this effort is important, we urge you to take a look at the video created by the World Economic Forum. (Go to Facebook and search "7 must have skills for children #wef".) The skills our young people today need are not the same as those required of us when we were their age. Take a look at the seven skills the World Economic Forum identifies:

- Critical Thinking and Problem Solving
- Collaboration and Leading by Influence
- Agility and Adaptability
- Initiative and Entrepreneurship
- Good Oral and Written Communication

- Assessing and Analyzing Information
- Curiosity and Imagination

REVOLUTION@ARY REFLECTION

How is your classroom's or school's focus similar to this graphic? How is it different?

We are not just talking about students who will find themselves at a shiny tech startup. We're talking about all students, no matter the field of work they enter after high school. We cannot think of a business or school, or virtually any other venture, that does not need problem solvers. The demand is high for these skills, but are we cultivating them in our learners today? Are we keeping these skills in mind when we conduct kindergarten or eighth grade assessments? Are we keeping them in mind when we're communicating with parents about their children's strengths? Are we considering these skills when we're preparing fifth-graders to succeed in middle school?

Harnessing Empathy

We believe middle school learners have great potential to solve the world's problems. In fact, all K–12 learners have this potential. If you want to spend all your time and energy simply producing great test takers and regurgitators, you should probably skip the rest of this chapter. Compliant behavior can be a lifelong pursuit for many. A quiet classroom in rows is great for teachers who need control, but it does little to help learners know how to treat one another or develop real interest and concern for their classmates or neighbors. Today's complex work environments demand more of people than compliant behavior. When we conduct an interview for a job, we don't look for hardcore obedience; we look for people who are personable and can see multiple angles. We need real problem solvers and collaborators. CEOs and hiring managers are not concerned about test scores. They are looking for learners who can adapt and have had revolution@ry learning experiences.

We want our students to have the ability to revolutionize the world, to reframe problems and build solutions that will improve the world. To do that they will need to understand the power of creating connections and the power of a collective intelligence. We need learners who understand all the dimensions of a problem and the multiple viewpoints of the user so that empathy can be achieved. The old paradigm of simply solving a word problem in front of a learner is done; now we need learners to connect with people in all aspects of the problem, articulate different viewpoints, and thoughtfully design solutions that will have long-term benefits for everyone.

We need empathetic learners.

REVOLUTION@ARY REFLECTION

How have you seen test-taking produce more agile learners? How does standardized testing improve curiosity and imagination? How does it stifle those traits?

Because we are middle school administrators, we often hear: "Middle school kids are going through so many emotions. It takes a special person to teach middle school!" Middle schoolers receive a bad rap today. To be honest, elementary and high school kids get one as well. Many of the middle schoolers we are around each day exhibit a high level of empathy. While we believe all K–12 students have a high level of empathy, we ardently believe that middle school learners have a growing fire to get behind a cause, to find something to believe in. They are a few years removed from a primary school setting, where they are trying to get the approval of the adult, and are now beginning to build social circles and ask questions about themselves. Some of you might be thinking, "Yeah, right! You don't have (fill in the blank), who sits in the classroom doing nothing every day." We don't dispute that you have unmotivated students—we all do. We just believe we can ask more of our students. We can expect great things from our students, and one of the first steps towards this is devoting time, effort, and resources to building empathy.

Our learners have a capacity for learning and demonstrating high levels of empathy; we just haven't allowed them to connect with it. This section is about a new way to learn. You cannot connect learners to an experience with the same worksheet that has been used the past ten years. They need a connection! They need a relevant experience. They need a revolution@ry teacher to spark that fire. They need you!

Why are we dedicating time to talk about empathy? We discuss it because we have seen that empathy can be a catalyst to learning. When their empathy chord is struck, learning is driven by curiosity and a goal to create change and solve problems. As yeast is to dough, empathy is to learning. Are you making a point to create conversations and learning opportunities for students to explore and understand empathy and compassion?

Idea Foundry

Thanks to the inspiration of Don Wettrick, we have created our own innovation class at HSMS. The creation of this course was spurred by numbers. We needed another exploratory offering to bring down class sizes in multiple electives, such as Spanish, Robotics, and Art. I (Darren) co-taught this innovation course with Carla Diede

(@CarlaDiede), and it was built with design thinking as the framework. To be honest, this has been the most enjoyable teaching experience! Seeing the passion and drive in our learners to make a difference is amazing. At different levels in the educational system, this approach can be called Genius Hour, passion projects, etc. I do want to note that even Carol Dweck believes that using the word "genius" to label a class suggests a fixed mindset. We wanted a different name to fit the learning environment. After checking with some leaders in the area of design thinking and entrepreneurship, we named the class Idea Foundry.

Idea Foundry is a hybrid of Don's work and the Design Thinking process from Stanford University. We encourage kids in this course to define and solve a specific problem, create a better world, or dig deeper into a passion. They "ideate," language we have them use, and design a prototype in our makerspace. The culmination of the project is testing the prototype, and in Idea Foundry, this step involves presentation.

The objective has been set for collaboration and ideation. The task in front of a group of eleven- and twelve-year-olds is to create a better school experience. Did you put the pieces together? I am the building principal allowing, no, expecting kids to tell me what is wrong with their school and educational experience. To begin this project, we model how a learner supports big and small ideas, the value of whiteboarding, and using the makerspace to produce artifacts.

After the learners have selected their topic, they empathize with their school experience; they interview one another to form a problem statement. I have had educators tell me they have used this model at the elementary level with success. It is simple and enlightening at the same time. Once the problem is identified, learners prepare for one of my favorite activities—whiteboarding. You can do this activity on most desks, small whiteboards, and glass windows. At HSMS we invested in Z-Racks and placed polymetal between the frames. There is great power in standing, talking, writing, and moving.

The "Create a better school experience" project was created so learners could empathize with an issue and solve a problem in our building. Once they get the cue to begin whiteboarding, the real magic happens. The low buzz of voices combined with dry erase markers moving is sweet music. Kids love solving problems. Kids love knowing their ideas matter! You see, this is real. This isn't a class I saw at some school and am writing about—we are living it and seeing the amazing results from kids being empowered to drive learning. People connected to the Target Corporation do this same activity in their teams and excitedly explain that they have seen the incredible results of it as well. It is powerful!

Five Tiles of Design Thinking

Design thinking is a building block for the entrepreneurial mindset at South Middle School. Several of our staff went to Stanford University for the training. We were encouraged to apply to the d.school for K–12 educators a few years ago. We chose this model because of the structure it provides kids to develop and present projects. Our goal was to take a team to facilitate change in our school. At first I used this model when we returned to our school as a way to gain feedback from our learners on our programs and initiatives. As you will see repeatedly in this book, we believe schools often fail to tap into our most important stakeholders: our learners. The feedback I received was profound, and I was left dumbfounded by the logical input from our kids. But I had been waiting to take the Design Thinking model to a new level.

The Design Thinking model is a proven process from Stanford that brings structure to solving problems. Our team knew about the five-tiled model, but the two-day workshop brought the concepts to life. The five tiles are empathize, define, ideate, prototype, and test.

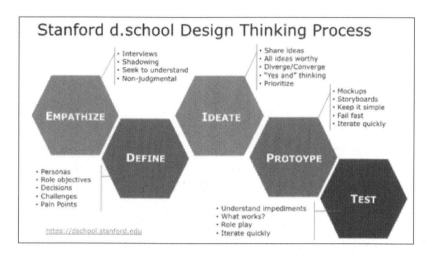

Source: What Is Design Thinking and Why Is It So Popular?
https://buff.ly/2q7ILjo

Here's a closer look at the Design Thinking process from Stanford University:

Empathize—This is the initial step required to engage in the design process, and it is the most important stage. You must be able to empathize with the user. I believe this generation has a high level of empathy, but we must provide opportunities for them to engage. If they get engaged, they become immersed in the empowerment level.

Define the Problem—Once you have empathized with the user or people affected, you pinpoint the problem to address. Your learners might need help pinpointing a problem. In our experience defining the problem can easily be confused with looking for a possible solution.

Ideate—In my opinion this is the most rewarding and enjoyable stage. This step is when you list ANY idea or solution to the problem. Big and crazy ideas are encouraged. Those ideating also need to use language like "Yes, and…" to promote the ideas of the community.

Prototype—Building a prototype is another great creative step in the design process. In our case learners use our makerspace and materials found in it. Prototypes can be digital, but the most rewarding projects are made from LittleBits, drones, or plain-old cardboard. Our prototyping cart, which we copied from the d.school, has been invaluable. It houses a variety of supplies on multiple shelves.

Test—In our school the testing step is the final presentation. I have learned, though, that there should be several iterations before the final test. We believe strongly in providing our students with guidance and assistance as they evaluate and revise, and we do this primarily in two ways:

- Including adults within and outside the school building to provide feedback loops—feedback that can clarify a confusing point or resolve an unfinished thought.
- Foam board. Yes, the same material used by contractors and home builders. We use large sheets as storyboards so feedback can be visual, where the ideas are placed on Post-It notes so they can be easily arranged.

Empathy and Problem Solving: Connect with the World

In order to develop an empathetic mindset, a person has to obtain knowledge from the user's standpoint. The "Create a Better School Experience" project was just a one-week, introductory task for our kids. The remainder of their time in this class was wide open to their ideas. We have discovered an amazing recipe by combining empathy with learner interests. Their ideas and methods for empathizing with their problems were original, mind-blowing, and would never have been brought to light if they weren't allowed to think for themselves.

Before we let the learners go through the empathy stage, they need to understand how they will do it. We spend time with them developing questions and prompts so they are prepared to speak or interview local or global experts. Things as simple as role playing how to write an email that asks for assistance, rehearsing how to ask permission to speak to someone over the phone, and using questions that promote multiple answers are stressed.

We also want our learners to connect with an expert related to their project for two reasons. First, we want our learners to understand the skill of connecting. This will be a necessary skill in their future as the use and capability of technology grows. They need to learn about and understand the power of collective intelligence. Second, the best resource to learn about the problem and solutions is speaking with someone who has experienced the environment or situation. This approach helps define the problem they will research.

At South MS our learners are connecting with community members and people around the world. How do we find them? This is my favorite task when helping with this class. First, know that you do not need to look far to find experts. They are in your school, community, and state. I have even used the head of maintenance in our building as an expert for several projects. In our area of South Dakota, we have an entrepreneurial network and organization called Zeal. Periodically, they will come to our school and provide input, connections, and/or be the expert for a project to engage empathy.

Experts are in your social networks. While I was writing this section of the book, I leveraged my social media network to have speaker/keynoter Kevin Carroll help a few boys who were passionate about designing athletic shoes. Kevin, who was the Play Coordinator for Nike, connected them with a designer at PENSOLE Footwear Design Academy.

Another group of boys wanted to map the areas covered by state conservation officers to halt poachers. Because phone numbers were listed on the state website, they empathized and received more passion for their cause when they called and asked questions of these officers. They called more than twenty officers who helped them hypothesize whether or not the state had enough officers to stop poaching. If you are wondering how long it took to make those phone calls, it took three to four class periods. And it was worth it. The data they received was invaluable. The stories they heard were insightful. Moreover, learning how to address adults appropriately, ask open-ended questions, and handle rejection when someone declines to talk were all real-world skills and experiences that will only help them in the future.

Whether local or worldwide, we need to utilize these connections to provide authentic learning for our kids. You would be surprised how often experts will come to your school, take a phone call, or video chat with your kids. Our learners have talked to scientists from Turkey and Harvard. They have made connections with local lawmakers to understand how their ideas could push legislation. Don't be pessimistic or choose to focus only on the standards you can cover. It should be obvious they are learning about subjects like communication and presentation skills, science related to plastic pollution with environmental studies, and local government procedures, to name a few. There is no prescribed curriculum that fits each person in this class, and I believe teaching with that reality in mind is revolution@ry. And it can be replicated in every classroom.

The Struggle

The struggle is real. I have felt it personally and for my learners at HSMS. If you are still struggling to find experts to connect with your learners, find a few people with a large network that love to connect. Even though Don Wettrick is busy, he taps his network for the right match with our Idea Foundry projects. I want to speak about these contacts. They want to help kids. An entrepreneur in Don's network talked to one of our girls about becoming an entrepreneur. These professionals have a growth mindset, and they can help our kids learn to connect and collaborate.

What do you do if your request of an expert is rejected? Move on. There are too many people and resources in our world today to let a failure like this stop you. Persistence has to be prominent in our DNA, and we have to teach this same persistence to our learners. We have to help them learn how to persist. We have to break down whatever previous structures of formal education exist so their potential can take root.

I have a passion for history, especially World War II history. I become completely engaged in the strategy of battle, the causes of conflict, and the people who have shaped history. The shapers are particularly interesting to me when they display undying persistence. Take Winston Churchill, a leader who was not England's first choice to lead the country during the war. As Winston Churchill stated, "A pessimist sees the difficulty in every opportunity; an optimist sees the opportunity in every difficulty." What about our kids? Are we instilling this grit and drive in them? We can speak for our schools. We are trying as hard as we can.

Define

It is through the empathy stage that learners find their problem to be solved. We have discovered that you need to help them see the difference between the problem and the solutions. A portion of our learners want to jump right to the solutions in the ideate stage, so we back them up and help them define the problem first. This stage requires intentional 1-on-1 reflection so they have a viable jumping-off point for the excitement that is Ideation.

One example involves two sixth-grade girls combining their passions: women's rights and immigrants in our area. They merged their thoughts into one problem statement: Mistreatment of Nepalese Women. Their problem statement was linked to one of the highest immigrant populations in our area, and their research focused on comparing the trials in their native country to what they experience in the United States. That is a heavy topic for sixth graders, but they came up with some amazing solutions.

Ideate

We teach our middle school students to use language intentionally. It is very common to hear them use words and phrases like "ideation," "prototype," "empathize with the user," "user/designer relationship," etc. Don't allow outdated beliefs or language that communicates low expectations of kids to reside in your work. If they are challenged and taught to use design thinking language, kids will do it. This applies to elementary, middle school, and high school learners.

When we have learners ideate solutions to their problem during Idea Foundry, we use a room full of whiteboards. There are mounted whiteboards and rolling whiteboards that use Z-Racks. After we model the brainstorming process for students, we let them go. The results have been amazing! I have video proof of their thoughtful ideation, which I believe is revolution@ry for sixth graders. As they begin to ideate, we also play music. We wondered if the music would distract them, so we normed the process. The success rate of focused inventors was nearly 100 percent. They rocked it! Research shows that low- to medium-level noise boosts creativity. I use Amazon playlists labeled for creative work or a selection of songs from Apple Music. To be able to stand, write, and listen during this time juices the process. It is special!

While they are brainstorming, I have learned to bring in as many adults as possible. Some of you are thinking, "With music playing and twenty-five kids talking at the same time, I bet you need help supervising." Uh, not even close. I have adults in there for two reasons. First, I want many experienced minds present to help refine ideas. We all need different perspectives, and the adults provide feedback without creating ideas for the kids. Second, the adults are there to find connections to experts for the projects.

After the solution is selected, we move the group to the makerspace to begin the prototype stage. Their experts could still be involved in this stage. We emphasize that this is an iterative process, one in which we are always working to improve on the previous prototype. Ideating is ongoing. Feedback is crucial for them. Even if they don't seek out feedback, the facilitator still provides it to them.

Prototype

During the prototype stage, we utilize our makerspace area to build, create, and design their prototypes. Their prototype is designed to match the solution from the ideate stage. Learners have the opportunity to use STEM tools (Makey-Makey, drones, etc.), cardboard, art supplies, and other materials from our prototyping cart, or they can harvest parts from our tear-apart area. In some cases, it involves creating a website or an app. As long as it brings their solution into reality, it doesn't matter what materials are used. Just create and be authentic. Make it your own, we tell them. We encourage the learners to have a draft of their prototype on paper as the first step in the planning process.

One example involved a team of girls with a passion to help animals. They worked with our local Humane Society to solve a paperwork problem. During the empathy stage, the girls discovered that when someone went to the Humane Society, it would typically take thirty to forty-five minutes to complete paperwork. Their solution and prototype was to create an application that provided people access to the paperwork online from the Humane Society's website.

Another example involved two boys who explored the use of drone technology to complete farming tasks such as tilling and combining. Using a few of our flying drones, they prototyped how this would work with different attachments that they created to add to the drones. Through the empathy stage, they even had pricing calculated for fuel cells, attachments, and the drone itself. It was very impressive.

But these prototypes can be made with simple items you have in your school. Cardboard has to be our most used commodity. Two girls wanted to tackle plastic pollution, specifically plastic bottle recycling. They prototyped a bottle deposit machine by making it out of cardboard. It was life-sized and decorated and served the purpose for the test phase.

Test and Feedback

The test phase of the design process involves a formal presentation. We allow the kids to make the decision on how they present: poster board, slides, skit, etc. One item that has to be a part of the presentation is the prototype. We want something that can be physically presented to the group and any adults who may be watching. To make this presentation more formal, we invite family and other adults to attend. By the time they present, we make sure they have had two or more feedback sessions, which we call feedback loops, on their project. We have learned that they need help closing that feedback loop.

What Are the Benefits of Design Thinking?

The main benefit of design thinking for educators is that this model uses a framework that is easy to understand and apply. Depending on the grade level, teachers can adjust design thinking to fit specific needs and ultimately empower their students' thoughts and actions. Another benefit is empathy. The core value of design thinking is empathy. Through the Idea Foundry and our iChoose projects at South Middle

School, we have discovered that while our students have a high level of empathy, they need open-minded educators to help them apply that empathy to problems and passions that resonate with them.

I won't withhold any truths from you. As I expected, we had some learners who didn't connect to Genius Hour projects or who couldn't find any issues they wanted to tackle. They would say, "I don't have a passion." A certain percentage of them would also disengage and just watch other people complete their projects. We had that happen with our Genius Hour projects. But the number of students who had trouble engaging in the design thinking process is zero. There is 100 percent participation. In my experience, design thinking allows you to intervene with designed feedback and reflection. Remember, some students are conditioned to "think" a certain way in schools, following the old method that produces robotic attitudes for an industrial model that is obsolete. We need to break them from these attitudes.

I will tell you that we have witnessed more successful outcomes in these projects by persisting and not allowing our students to maintain a fixed mindset. One example involved two sixth-grade learners, Bram and Marshall, who could not find a problem to solve. They were moving in and out of several ideas. When we persisted in emphasizing the frames of empathy and finding a passion, the light came on! Their final product was an impact sensor created from LittleBits that they placed in an old football helmet. The sensor alerted training staff if impact to the helmet was strong enough for a possible concussion. Their expert, who worked at a local athletic facility, told them they had developed the next generation in monitoring concussions. #micdrop

The Future Is Today

Think back to the findings of the World Economic Forum. How many of those seven skills are present in Idea Foundry or any model based on design thinking?

- Critical Thinking and Problem Solving
- Collaboration and Leading by Influence
- Agility and Adaptability
- Initiative and Entrepreneurship
- Good Oral and Written Communication
- Assessing and Analyzing Information
- Curiosity and Imagination

All of them! Idea Foundry and similar courses are based on problem solving. Kids are collaborating with one another in groups and with people all over the world. Leading by influence? This type of class destroys the top-down approach to learning and empowers kids to drive their own learning. They become the influencers. Agility? Kids learn to pivot or adjust their thinking to solve the problem in front of them. Imagination? Watch a learner create a helmet out of KNEX and tell me imagination isn't present during prototyping.

I have two children in the elementary stage of education, and I pay attention to their test scores like any parent. We have all been trained (or brainwashed) to believe these scores have monumental importance. But when I help them with homework or talk about their school day, I emphasize persistence, hard work, creativity, and growth mindset qualities. I want my children to be imaginative and agile thinkers, capable of creating solutions to problems that fit an entrepreneurial mindset. We can't ignore the future. The future is today. Let's launch the revolution.

A Human-Centered Approach to Learning by Revolution@ry Educator Mary Cantwell (@scitechyEDU) (DEEPDESIGNTHINKING.COM)

Design thinking is a human-centered approach to learning, creating, and being through empathy. It is a way to solve wicked and simplistic problems, design new ways of doing things, and to view the world around you with an empathetic lens.

I am a firm believer that the term "Teacher" can also mean "Design Thinker." As teachers we are called to share, expose, empathize, collaborate, connect, relate, create, problem-solve, instruct, and design for our students on a daily basis. A design thinker is called to share, expose, empathize, collaborate, relate, connect, create, problem-solve, instruct, and design for their End-User. The real difference between these two sentences is the framed noun, student and end-user. They are one and the same, yet in context, they are distinguished simply to serve a specific demographic.

I can see how awareness, intentionality, and action can play a huge role in the infusion of design thinking and its daily practice in an educational environment. As teachers become more aware of the common language, the power of the mindsets, and how design thinking is more than just a framework to follow, their view of their students, their learning spaces, and every other aspect of "school" changes. It is then that their intentions will create a shift and a stronger pivot towards designing for their End-Users (students) on a minute-by-minute basis. Now awareness and intention can easily be shoved in the corner as papers pile up, pressure mounts for, say, grades and results, and the daily grind of teaching takes ownership of your actions. It's great to be mindful, but it is better to demonstrate mindful action that puts the end-user at the forefront to drive the learning, creating, and being in the classroom.

On February 26, 2010, I learned about this thing called design thinking. I learned of an outstanding educator named Kim Saxe who was using design thinking as an approach to teaching and learning with her students at The Nueva School. I also learned that Stanford University had a learning space dedicated to all things Design Thinking called the d.school. It was on this day of learning about DT that a huge portion of my instructional practices and beliefs found a home where I could gain a better understanding of and confidence in my pedagogy and learning. For the next year and a half, I devoured, explored, researched, and stalked Kim's work and the d.schools' multiple online resource offerings and constantly Googled to find more knowledge around design thinking.

I created and designed a process I coined DEEP in May of 2010: Discover, Empathize, Experiment, Produce. The common language, ease of use, and the obvious emphasis on Empathy was the cornerstone of my design. And from the beginning, after completing the six-week pilot design thinking challenge, I have always intentionally strived to "infuse" DEEP design thinking throughout the learning environment.

I am confronted with things all over the place, things that stand solo and disconnected from all the other things we encounter in life. With DEEPdt, I don't want it to be just another thing, and I especially do not want it to be a solo, disconnected thing. While I understand there are countless others, my approach is to infuse design thinking into the daily life of students and teachers. If we lead with empathy in our Users, how can we go wrong? People-centered is where I want us to start...and stay. This is an easy answer, and it's even easier to understand why others don't see how this is possible, yet.

DEEPdt is just one way of many to solve a problem, yet the clear difference is that it's people-centered. It is the User who defines the real problem and leads us to the solution. The true gift of having our students utilizing and practicing design thinking approaches in our classrooms is that they will have a stronger and more impactful empathetic posture when they walk out of your classroom and encounter life as it is—messy, sad, joyful, difficult, challenging, cruel, beautiful, and, most of all, full of diverse and amazing people.

There are little bits of every day that could be redesigned, and then there are bigger, meatier, and messier chunks of life that are full of problems and needs to tackle. In keeping with this reality, the infusion of DEEPdt into the school environment can come in bits or chunks. What's most important is our awareness, intentionality, and actions as educators towards our students.

CALL TO ACTION

▶ Rethink learning and reevaluate the curriculum used in your classroom or school. Is it helping you empower your learners?

▶ Why do you believe there is value (or no value) in creating future entrepreneurs?

▶ How can you use the design thinking process in your classroom or school to solve problems?

▶ How can you create learning experiences that harness your students' passions?

CHAPTER 7

CREATE A MAKER REVOLUTION

WE'RE GOING TO TAKE a slightly different approach to the career talk.

If your K–12 experience was like ours, then you remember career day visits and surveys and talks that became progressively specific to help you narrow your career path. The goal for all our well-intentioned educators was to help us make a decision about what we would do as a career for the rest of our lives!

When I (Derek) was a sophomore in high school, my career interest survey yielded two exciting options: pilot and computer programmer. If you know me, you know I was jumping out of my skin to fly a plane, but a discouraging talk with a recruiter about my height, of all things, quickly extinguished my piloting dreams. I guess they thought I couldn't reach the gas pedal.

Nonetheless, I was still excited to learn about computer programming, and I left high school to study in that field. Much later I realized I really didn't want to program computers or even know how they worked. I just enjoyed seeing what they could do. But that realization didn't stop me from thinking I was a failure for not living up to what should have been my one path in life. Lots of confusion and bewilderment later ensued when I discovered a passion for political science, specifically Third World studies. Exposure to African American studies really changed my life, leading me to earn a minor in the field.

Exploring something I was passionate about made me happy. I spoke with enthusiasm about African politics and history and African-American history. It grounded me later in life and gave me the option to fall back on an earlier passion when I started teaching middle school math.

My own winding road to teaching has taught me a great deal about helping students explore the many different paths their lives can take. Instead of trying to narrow down career choices for learners early in their lives, we should be focused on building up the skills they will need to become curious, adaptable problem solvers. We must focus on helping students realize they can and should be passionate about certain things, and that there is danger in simply going through the motions.

My children are older than Darren's—my 24-year-old daughter is a psychology major and my 29-year-old son just passed the bar. It has been amazing watching them grow up and observing the parallels and differences in their approaches to adulthood.

REVOLUTION@ARY REFLECTION

Is the passion we instill in learners going to serve them as future citizens and problem solvers? Are our learners going to be good people from our intentional efforts?

First, they are both focused on being good people. We are so proud of who they are striving to be and the friends they have. Did their schools have that focus? What would my kids say?

Second, they are both more skilled at more things than I could have imagined. They each know coding and some knowledge about computer hardware. My daughter learned Japanese from YouTube (I would love to tell you the story of her going to Japan). They are truly digital natives and love to question, challenge, and then look it up to get it done. My favorite example of this digital mindset was a dinner conversation during which they both revealed that during high school they were probably assigned, collectively, only six books to read. That's right. Six. Of course I was floored. This revelation blew my mind and made me question what was going on in our house of educators. My mind raced with questions, the first of which was, "OMG, can my kids read?" Then I jumped to, "How could they graduate high school and college with honors—summa cum laude and a Presidential Award— with that kind of reading list?" Their answer was a sentiment that I share often: if you can web search the answer, then it's the wrong question.

- Were my kids prepared for life?
- Are they equipped for what comes next?

The answer doesn't lie in a literature grade (even though I'm still looking at that work); it comes from the values and qualities that we as parents and teachers were building up in them throughout school.

The Danger of Learned Helplessness

Compliant workers looking for direction at every turn will not have a future in tomorrow's job market. With more and more jobs being automated, employers will need workers who can create solutions and questions to help them think differently. Automation will take care of the routine tasks, but where does that leave your students in the next ten to fifteen years? STEM careers in an automated world do not need minimum-wage workers.

Teacher-centered practices give a lot of direction and don't allow much growth or exploration for learners. How can students learn negotiation and critical thinking if their only requirements are to raise their hands and produce an answer every day in class?

These practices and thinking breed a learned helplessness in our students, wherein learners wait on the teacher for direction instead of taking the initiative to act. While this approach might serve a teacher who has control issues, it will do little to help an employee who's new to a management role. Facilitating this learned helplessness is a disservice to a learner's future. Have you ever heard a fellow teacher tell students not to move or ask questions until they were directed to? That mindset is not only a direct obstacle to authentic learning, it's also impractical. How can students learn to be agile thinkers and develop cognitive flexibility when even their thoughts and movements are dictated? They can't.

We interviewed a hero of ours, Barbara Bray (@bbray27), to talk about student agency and we walked into the great topic of learned helplessness. According to Bray, the current educational system was designed for teachers to control and manage the learning. This system continues today because teachers are the ones held accountable and responsible for the learning instead of the learners. Too often adults treat children as though they are incapable of making decisions or holding valid opinions. As children advance through the system, they develop a form of "learned helplessness" that keeps them from advocating for themselves. The process for learning and the role learners play must be different than what most adults experienced when they were in school.

REVOLUTION@ARY REFLECTION

Do you look for safe answers or directions instead of being willing to take a risk?

This shift is not needed because young people are learning less than previous generations. In fact, there is good evidence that they know much more. The forces behind this shift are the rapid and ever-increasing pace of change, the complexity of the world in which we live, and the unpredictability of what people will need to know in the coming decades. This is the future for which we need to prepare today's learners.

As educators, we must nurture, coach, and build into our learners a greater capacity to initiate, manage, and maintain their own learning. Learning will be a constant and high-priority activity throughout their lives, and they will need the skills and tools to manage this process.

Think of your classroom or school. Do you want to prepare students for a factory-model job that will be obsolete in the next five years or give them the skills they need to thrive in the world ahead? Educators can no longer deliver content in a decades-old manner and still expect students to function in 2019. Even for adolescents and teenagers, daily life has become far more complex, and the skills they need to navigate middle school and high school are changing rapidly.

We have to be willing to embrace learning that can be messy and that comes with a little bit of crazy. Opportunities to revolutionize teaching do exist today. There are pockets of this kind of innovation across our country and the world. Are you ready to join in?

Creating a Maker Culture

Every school leader has a culture they are working to establish. We select particular attributes we want our learners to reflect, then we emphasize specific ways of learning and use specific tangible materials to help build the culture over time. At South Middle School, I (Darren) have emphasized a maker culture based on creativity and innovation. Our school is committed to providing students with multiple opportunities to make and create. Stanford's d.school has a sign that states, "There's Only Make." It resonates strongly with my team. To facilitate this maker culture at South Middle, we created a makerspace in our library.

Makerspaces, along with STEM/STEAM initiatives, have arrived, and the benefits to learners are proven and visible. Allowing learners to make places them in the driver's seat, and the places they go are bound to boggle the mind!

How to Create a Makerspace

A makerspace is a designated area that is equipped with a combination of tools to allow learners to explore, build, and create. Laura Fleming, whom many consider the pioneer of the makerspace movement, says, "A school makerspace is a metaphor for a unique learning environment that encourages tinkering, play, and open-ended exploration for all."

For South Middle School, makerspaces provide an opportunity to make a dream or passion come to life. Like many schools, our makerspace is our library, and we encourage a lot of collaboration in this space. (Makerspaces can be found in a variety of locations and feature tools that range from pricey and high-tech to old-school and inexpensive.) To make this jump in a library setting, your library or media center leaders must be willing to embrace noise and, at times, messy learning. We still have books in our library, but many of the areas have been restructured to promote making.

Carving out our makerspace didn't happen overnight, but we knew it would be a critical step in establishing the maker culture we wanted at South Middle. Here are the key steps we recommend for those looking to give it a try:

Start with a vision. Gather the individuals at your school who desire the change. Without that shared vision for learning, the maker items will end up dusty and unused. At HSMS, Travis Lape (@travislape) and Kristi Jones (@KristiJ1102) helped me create a robust maker environment. Determine why you want or need a makerspace.

Resolve to make it fun. Learners need to feel that the makerspace is their space. It's a space where they don't have to worry about clean, orderly learning. Their thoughts are valued, and experimentation is always allowed.

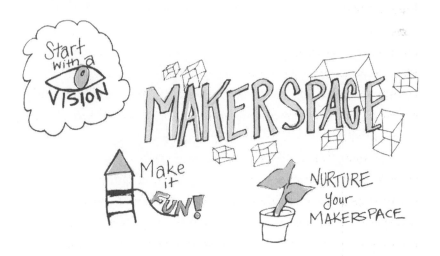

Nurture your makerspace. Enlist the help of people who are interested and passionate about creating. They might not be a perfect fit, but it's always important to have the support of people who embrace continuous building, playing, and exploring.

Our makerspace had humble beginnings with easy-to-use STEM/STEAM tools. A Makey-Makey invention kit was our first purchase, and over the next few months we added other tools such as Snap Circuits, LittleBits, and some 3D printers. Next, we added Osmo, Spheros, and Ozobots. Our learners flocked to the library, eagerly tinkering and experimenting with these new materials. Many students came in early before school and stayed late in the afternoon to continue their projects, and they still do today!

How about a Drone Club? Why Not!

In the fall of 2015, I started our Drone Club at HSMS based on interest from our kids. We begin at 7:00 a.m. so the kids with activities after school can participate. Although I thought attendance might be high, 7:00 a.m. is early. I was pleasantly surprised when we had more than thirty participants, with groupies following the crowd. We began by flying and driving drones. The driving drones could also jump, which added some great internal innovations.

We used our library/makerspace area as our space inside the building. As interest grew, we created a Drone Room that still houses all our drones to this day. It has also become a space where we create race tracks and obstacle courses. I have allowed the kids to own the space, and they take great pride in it. I even have a group of kids that design ways to store and charge the drones.

In the beginning, most of the learners were boys in grades six through eight. This demographic group seemed to be typical as I talked with other schools involved in the drone movement. The only permission they needed to participate was the form for the club. We meet weekly for ten weeks in a semester. Many semesters we end up meeting even more because of the high level of interest. To this day, I still have kids show up at school at 7:00 a.m. asking for the space to be opened for them to "work."

Eventually we started some drone challenges and recorded them for other groups to copy. Drone challenges required learners to create courses, tracks, or tricks for their peers to complete. Drones were flying through hoops, under tables, or racing against each other. Jumping drones were put to the test by going from the floor to higher elevations. We expanded our footprint by posting to Brad Gustafson's #edudronechallenge as well as participating in drone challenges against area schools.

Our Drone Room had humble beginnings. We started with a few Parrot driving and flying drones. As interest grew, we realized we needed a designated area for our drones, and we called it the Drone Room. In our collection we have driving, jumping, and flying drones from five different companies. The goal is to bring learners to this space and enjoy an experience. This experience with our drones might be the only time a slice of our students has the opportunity to use one.

As the technology progressed, we began to code drones. Today, coding drones has never been easier. There are few things more rewarding than seeing a learner problem solve a maze or situation. The intensity in their focus is awe-inspiring. Recently we developed the Drone Olympics in honor of the summer and winter Olympics. Events mimicked sprints, hurdles, relays, and whatever the learners could create. During this forty-five-minute fly or drive time, learners can operate drones for the first time, obtain a license (an idea from one of our learner experts), or compete in challenges. Check out my Twitter handle, @dellwein, to see some of the adventures.

What I love most about our Drone Club gatherings are the ideas from the kids. Their creativity is endless. A group of boys decided we needed to create a procedure to obtain a license before using certain functions of the drones. They led courses during iChoose (Chapter 8) to teach proper use and care of the drones. It was brilliant, and it was all learner-generated. We gave them a few presentation tips, but their empowered spirits knocked this idea out of the park. Empowered learning is the key to leading a revolution.

No Money, No Problem

If money is on your mind, there are many inexpensive maker tools available for purchase. To be honest, the most used materials in our makerspace have virtually no cost at all— cardboard and donated PVC pipe. Our learners love to create prototypes with cardboard. (And talk about a resource that is prevalent in a school!) What a great way to learn, fail, and start over. Some of our best projects are completed with neglected cardboard supplies. We have discovered that our kids will happily use most any material at their disposal.

Here's another tip: don't throw away those old hard drive towers. At our makerspace Tear-Apart Station, our learners—you guessed it—tear them apart and reassemble them. Throwing out any of those automated towel dispensers? Our makers will scoop them up, harvest the motors, and use them for other automated projects. Old lamps? Unused radio-controlled cars? You might be surprised how many of your students would delight in fixing them or dismantling them to learn how they are built. Don't be scared to let them rip and play. This is revolution@ry learning!

Other maker tools that are relatively inexpensive include KEVA Planks and K'NEX. A group of our eighth-grade boys just finished an eight-foot Ferris wheel made out of K'NEX.

Check out my YouTube channel (Darren Ellwein) to see how they moved the structure to a dark room so its LED lights would be visible. When we Tweeted about this project, the feedback from elementary classrooms and STEM teachers was incredible. All of a sudden, their project had no walls, and the world could see their work. It even led them to create an improved version of the original structure. The possibilities are endless!

Girl Power

As I mentioned earlier, it wasn't as common for girls to come to Drone Club or our makerspace areas at first. To be honest, there were less than a handful per week coming to the makerspace. This disparity exists in the tech industry at large. Today at HSMS, girls are migrating to this space in numbers equal to or greater than the boys. This growth has been accomplished by encouraging them and placing items that interest them in our makerspaces. We intentionally added sewing machines (also donated) to draw them in, an effort that is being spearheaded by our Library/Media Specialist, Kristi Jones (@kristij1102). In general, though, our numbers for girl attendance have increased greatly just by having a prototyping cart.

This cart allows them to craft and create because all the materials are in one place. As I write this, we have twelve-year-old girls who have created a craft corner with repurposed and devalued items. At Christmas they decide to make their gifts instead of buying them. They bring mason jars and create vases or snow globes. They bring in building blocks and clothespins to make message boards for one another for their Secret Santa gifts. Someone brought an old jewelry box to school, which led to it being repurposed into an American Girl Doll dresser. One girl even created a backpack out of felt, cardboard, and zippers. Their ideas are just amazing! This is THEIR space, and they treasure the empowerment and ownership it provides. It makes no sense to employ a top-down authority in this day. We can have structure for learners while also awarding them ownership. Stop the "my way or the highway" attitude and work WITH your learners.

Even Drone Club has girl participation. If you have or plan to stock drones, you need to provide equal time for boys and girls. Boys naturally gravitate to drones, and I believe most people generalize that drones are only of interest to males. This is not true, however. I purposely set aside drones for our girls to fly or drive, and they loved it! I have a group of them that make a straight path to the flying drones and have become very skilled.

The Next Step

Many school leaders push back at the makerspace movement, questioning whether or not it's a good use of public funds. This is particularly true when these spaces don't directly correlate to the prescribed curriculum. My first response? Yes! These spaces are a great use of public funds. Any time we empower our kids to be passionate, we all win! Second, maker tools do align with the curriculum—you just have to take the time to see the connections. Since we launched our makerspace, we have been working to find ways to incorporate our maker tools into the curriculum. We believe their greatest value is realized when our learners connect the use of the tool with the curricular objective.

Making those connections, however, does require time. I have utilized in-service time to allow staff the time they need to play and find connections to their curriculum. The school leader, library-media specialist, or technology integrationist also needs to work side-by-side with the content teacher. Be intentional. If you desire a maker culture, you have to be ruthless about carving out the time. Here are some of our results in various content areas:

Math—Parrot Jumping Drones and the Pythagorean Theorem

Spanish—Spheros and explaining directions on a large town map

English/Language Arts—LittleBits and expository writing

Science—Stop-motion with LEGO bricks to show a journey to the center of the earth

The rich resources on my Twitter network produce examples of this learning on a daily basis. I even saw a recent post of students using Ozobots with Geometry. Revolution@ry teachers see the connection with a learner's current world and create opportunities for empowerment with these STEM materials. The point is this: I can provide a plethora of examples for incorporating maker items into the curriculum, but you need to grasp this and make it your own. Educators are brimming with creativity, but the system handcuffs leaders and classroom change agents. Get connected to like-minded colleagues on social media and grow yourself. That growth will empower your learners to be producers instead of consumers.

3D Printing, Robotics, and STEAM

Some of the most popular tools in our library/makerspace are our 3D printers. This technology continues to evolve and progress, and schools that don't have one are missing out on a tremendous resource. Don't worry about having to understand all the moving parts of the necessary software because kids are extremely intuitive in the process. Teachers at HSMS have found that 3D printers are perfect for projects in every content area. Many of our learners use them for prototypes during Idea Foundry.

If your school or library does not want to support this venture, then we encourage you to seek support on your own. Contact the company directly to see what offers or deals they might give you in return for promoting them on social media. All of these companies love to see kids using their products. Search for grants, or make a request on DonorsChoose.org. Show your determination to empower your classroom.

Many of these Maker tools are considered robotics. Drones, Spheros, and VEX also fit this category. What brings robotics to the next level is the coding with problem solving. Using pieces of software like Tynker, kids can program speed and distance. Sounds like math and science to me. Many companies now build their own applications to support their robotics. This program fits learning in the Science, Technology, Engineering and Mathematics (STEM) movement, which has grown in popularity and purpose in recent years.

STEAM is STEM with an added 'A' for Art. The arts have been neglected and on the chopping block for many schools in our country. STEAM has helped the Arts return. If you research #STEAM on Twitter, you will see artwork brought to life with Chatterpix. STEAM is also taking design concepts and pushing technology tools into the design process. You can design a cardboard car and make it mobile with maker tools. Makey-Makey can be coded and added to a diorama, painting, or drawing. Randi Murphy (@RandiKayMurphy) is an art teacher who uses Spheros for art projects. Since Spheros can be placed into tempera paint, she uses it to empower learners to control these round robots to create paintings. She has also used Osmo Masterpiece to bring a different twist to drawing.

Making It Mobile

It is entirely possible to have a makerspace that is not static. Many schools have made their maker materials mobile because they don't have a room to spare. Time is another reason for creating a mobile makerspace. Some teachers do not want to move learners to a separate space and lose instructional time. If you have a basic cart, the teacher can use it to easily move the maker materials. Almost any maker tool can be transported to a classroom. Our most recent example includes our Tear-Apart Station. Kids love to take apart old computers, speaker systems, or towel dispensers. Our maker kids even harvest parts, like motors, to use with their creations. Our English/language arts students will then use these parts to work on their expository writing skills by explaining the process or steps required to take them apart and put them back together.

As a school leader, you need to assess your comfort level with this environment. It is important to find staff to embrace a maker culture. I recommend following Twitter accounts in the makerspace world, along with #makerspace, #makered, and #stem hashtags, to list a few.

CALL TO ACTION

▶ What is holding you back from creating a maker culture in your classroom or school?

▶ What can you do now to make a shift toward this kind of culture?

▶ How can you incorporate maker items into your content area?

▶ What pitfalls will you encounter with a makerspace? How can you overcome these?

CHAPTER 8

EMPOWERING LEARNERS TO BE REVOLUTION@RIES

WE KNOW WHAT YOU are thinking when you read the title of this chapter: Darren and Derek, you guys have lost your minds! Do you really expect us to give the keys of the school to our students?

Short answer? Kinda.

Sharing decision making, choice, and providing opportunities for student input are different ways of thinking, particularly in a middle school classroom. Our own learning experience as professionals has been that high levels of control and rigidity are essential to successful classrooms and well-run schools. Even how we use the terms "structure" and "organization" can imply a degree of perceived control and imposed order. On days when you drive to work on fire to be a part of students' lives, do you ever think, "Wow, I can't wait to be a classroom manager?" We really, really hope not.

We believe all teachers go into education to be revolution@ries. We all want to make a difference. We don't come to school to create mediocre experiences with students—we want to be difference makers. When we made the decision to work with young people, we vowed to have open minds, view our profession with fresh eyes, and inspire and encourage the children in our charge. Thanks to the trappings of traditional teacher prep programs, our own K–12 experiences, and our government's misguided commitment to an antiquated educational system, somewhere along the way all of our revolution@ry intentions morphed into lifeless "teacher practices."

We need to shake them off!

If we don't, we might never see the real learners who walk the halls of our schools every day. If we continue to cling to the status quo, we might never be able to embrace learner-centered systems. It won't be easy. It's difficult to let go of these practices, particularly when we thrived in them. But it's vital! We must rediscover the revolution@ries we once were.

I (Derek) speak from real experience. In 1995, I started teaching math and remedial reading at Bear Creek Middle School. Though she didn't hire me, most of my formative learning as a teacher came from my then-principal, Dr. Sandra DeShazier. When I started, I brought the best of my own learning experiences from my previous teachers. I was strict until December, I was occasionally funny and entertaining (at least in my mind), I knew the math, and I assigned worksheets and homework on a regular basis. It wasn't until Sandra began to push me that I began to do things differently. I converted my classroom to an all-tables room, started using rubrics for most assignments, and chose projects that students could have fun with, such as building miniature playgrounds.

One of the biggest shifts happened when we started using graphing calculators. It sticks out in my memory because it was the year I taught my son in a seventh-grade Algebra 1 class. It was also one of the moments in my teaching career when I realized I was truly holding my students back. We were playing around with a graphing function, and I was carefully and meticulously walking them through the process of changing the coefficient of x to get a different slope for a line. I was interrupted by a student named Carrie who politely explained how to enter multiple equations to display multiple lines. I quickly realized she was the unofficial spokesperson for the group and that I was the last one to catch up.

I also realized the math problems they were given to do from the book were just plug-in problems. There was nothing to figure out, no productive struggle. All they had to do was complete the problems and turn them in.

I'm sure most of you have had a realization like this, and I'm sure you also felt it was unacceptable. I didn't like knowing that I was actually a barrier to a deeper learning experience for my students.

Learners Need Us to Make a Revolution@ry Leap

It is quite a leap for educators to begin unlearning so much of what they were taught as students and as new teachers. It's difficult to redefine what learner-centered experiences actually mean and look like in today's classrooms, but it has to happen if we are going to unlock the potential in our schools. It's hard to prioritize learner experiences when we don't allow for some flexibility in what we explore, how we explore it, and how we demonstrate learning.

This is about embracing a mindset shift and a need for skills development; in other words, it's about lifelong learning. To bring out the best in my students, we must continue to grow and develop ourselves.

We've talked a lot about the role of the adult in a chapter that focuses on the learners in our schools. That's because it's impossible to have one without the other. The most important person in the school building is the teacher. Students are the reason and purpose for our schools, but the teacher is the most important person there. While principals certainly try to have as many conversations as they can with students throughout the day, it's the hearts, minds, and words of the teacher that will have the biggest impact, positive or negative, on students. The impact of a teacher's day-to-day influence can't be overemphasized.

Students → Learners → Revolution@ries

We fervently believe we can create great schools for great communities by changing our focus. With intentional work and effort, we can shift our focus from the outdated three Rs towards what we want and need our future citizens to look like.

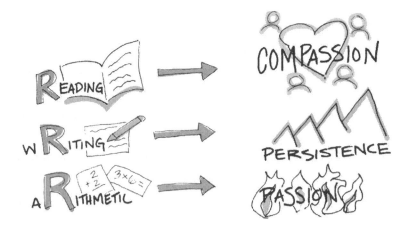

What characteristics do we want our middle schoolers to demonstrate?

What should their work ethic look like?

We don't believe certain students have a natural inclination towards reading or math or art. As we learn more about having a mindset focused on growth or achievement, we see the opportunity to emphasize characteristics we need to develop over a lifetime instead of focusing on standard learning topics. If we focus on creating active creatives who have a passion for something, e.g., art, algebra, or video production, then we will help unleash a creativity and focus that will change the world.

At HSMS, students who have adopted the mission of reducing the impact of plastic on the environment are changing how products are thought of, bought, and made by creating moving and powerful events for the community and school. At West Rowan Middle, students are on fire to bring awareness to animal rights causes and are going to great lengths to make sure awareness is kept on this need, and people all around them are willing to help their friends with these compassion projects. This is real passion that is nurtured. This can't be taught, but it can be grown and stirred to learning targets and change the world.

Active Creators or Passive Consumers

At HSMS we have a program spearheaded by staff called iChoose. What is it?

To provide our learners with the opportunity to be active content creators at HSMS, I (Darren) allowed several teachers to implement Genius Hour in their curriculum. Teachers would set aside one day a week for learners to work on whatever they wanted. This evolved into an entire building experience where each child had the opportunity to work on projects for one class period each week. The evolution continued after feedback, and today we have an experience called iChoose.

Presently iChoose is a combination of Edcamp offerings and project offerings we call Passion or Butterfly Effect projects. For the Edcamp option, we ask the kids what they want to learn. We take that information and create offerings in a schedule using software from personalizedlearningtools.com to account for each learner in this process. Kids can also sign up to work on a Passion project or a Butterfly Effect project (projects based on helping others or changing the world).

In the beginning we had teachers leading a variety of Edcamp offerings ranging from building a sports team with a salary cap to animal science sessions. Then a revolution@ry development began to take shape—our learners started leading offerings. With some guidance from our teachers, they created classes for their peers. They became the content creators for their own learning experiences. A group of girls created an American Sign Language (ASL) offering that continued for several weeks. We had three boys lead a Drone Certification offering, which we now use as a standard for our Drone Club.

We also relied on our community partnerships for Edcamp offerings. Their expertise on certain topics was well-suited to this concept of creators. Local coding companies offered their time so kids could create their own video games through coding. Another offering brought in an architect, and our kids had to create a floor plan for their "perfect" school. One of our popular offerings involved a local scuba diving company that integrated life science into their presentation.

Passion projects have had some great results when learners are given time to create. Learners created rock crystals after learning about them in earth science. Their project had many varieties of crystal formations and used different ingredients to test results. Another project involved a map of historic Harrisburg with 3D-printed buildings. The planning of the city itself took several weeks.

Butterfly Effect projects are a great opportunity to bring out empathy in kids. One of our projects involved autism awareness. Lauren, an eighth grader, developed a presentation with one of our learners who was on the autism spectrum and even presented her work at one of our state conferences. One of our Butterfly Effect projects saw two sixth-grade girls create their own Weebly website that highlighted two of their sixth-grade peers each week. In addition to posting photos, they wrote positive comments about each student. The best part? They did this without anyone knowing they were the authors of the project.

Compassion Project

It was proud work to develop our five core values at West Rowan Middle. These core values were inspired by our visit to Meadow Glen Middle, where we saw their Habits of Learning in action and how they permeated throughout school culture. While we didn't want to copy MGMS and replicate actions and procedures, we did want to think differently about how we framed conversations and planning around our middle schoolers. We began asking questions about what kind of learners and people we wanted our Bulldogs to be. It took us over half a year to get it right, but we finally came up with our core values. With input from students and staff, we decided on the following:

- Compassion
- Collaboration
- Communication
- Integrity
- Purpose

We developed lessons and activities around these traits and began embedding them into our daily experiences. Seeing integrity and purpose in our learning spaces meant we all had an understanding that we were going to be about meaningful and productive work. Seeing communication in action was a wonder. We began empowering learners to greet all visitors to the classroom and describe the learning goals and activities of the day, and we saw more and more presentations of student work and began talking about what high-level communication is.

From our brainstorming we came up with our Compassion Projects. Our mission for the Compassion Projects was simple: we wanted students to find ways to change a life, change their community, or change the world.

The only limitations we set were time frames. With massive organization from our counselors and assistant principals, students were able to choose their own topics and groups. Their facilitators guided their thinking by challenging them to take risks and think outside the box. They could do this independently or in small groups.

Every student and group had to present. Projects ranged in scope and output. They included:

- Reading to elementary school students
- Spending time with senior citizens
- Raising awareness and support for LGBT groups
- Hosting a fishing derby for a charity group
- Collecting food and supplies for local ministries
- Creating an event for veterans
- Volunteering time at food banks to prepare meals
- Collecting unused children's books to donate to a shelter

Changing the world is a revolution@ry enterprise.

Who Are These Revolution@ry Learners?

Based on our collective teaching and administrative experience, we have concluded that our middle school students are complex individuals who are setting themselves apart as leaders and learners in a rapidly-changing world (no surprise there). We've come up with some distinct commonalities of our "new middle school learners." Though we think this will apply to K–12 learners, we've seen these general attributes in our learners since we've begun the work of changing our culture and expectations. Moreover, our friends we've collaborated with have seen similar changes and traits. Though they come to our classrooms with a wide range of interests, habits, and opinions, the most common types of learners we see are:

- Goal Setters
- Collaborators
- Researchers
- Communicators

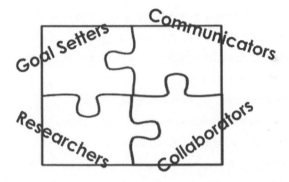

Goal Setters

In stark contrast to the model of being told what to learn and being given the conditions for how delivery will take place, learners begin to embrace and rely on opportunities to share their voice by setting goals for the trajectory of design and learning in the classroom. Revolution@ry educators can have great discussions with learners about setting worthy learning targets and make learner input a critical part of the discussion. Here are some questions to kick off the discussion:

- How can bringing in learner voices enhance learning?
- What are barriers to building a thriving culture of personalized learning in your school?
- What is your role in this?

Revolution@ry learners should be held accountable for the outcomes they set for themselves, and revolution@ry leaders should be willing to help them achieve their goals. Continuous monitoring and relationship building ensure learning is the priority, not deadline reinforcement. Many of our students have already started holding themselves accountable now. Our students begin setting high standards for being creative and for what they can complete. While observing two sixth graders completing a green screen weather forecasting project, I (Derek) thoroughly enjoyed listening in on these two young men having a very detailed discussion about script, the vocabulary they were going to use, and even the body position in front of the screen. This is the beauty of setting clear, high expectations in an environment of choice.

The only questions that may persist are how they will persevere when things get tough and what the adult's role is in that process. Changing who sets the goal won't change accountability, but it should have a great impact on how support is given.

Collaborators

Learning doesn't happen in a static, emotionless/motionless environment. Revolution@ry learners of ALL ages need to be involved in discussions, movement, and activities to make experiences part of the schema. For so long the game of school has been to remember something long enough for a test and then dump it when the next test comes around. This gaming doesn't prepare us for life.

Learning is social. We process more from interactions and working through difficulties and breakthroughs together. Planning for these experiences should be a part of our process, not something we avoid. We should model for learners how to build norms and work together. Learning how to follow expectations set by others is a lifelong need and one we start teaching early on, but do we help students build norms and expectations for the different groups they have to work in?

Consider the value of allowing students to provide voice or even drive the process of building norms and classroom expectations for what happens when the teacher is talking or for what behavior should be during group work time. Allowing them to be a part of the process is likely to yield great buy-in from all students, and it would be less reteaching expectation and more reminding and/or participating in the group discussion.

Researchers

In this information age, it's easy to get answers to simple questions (remember: if we can web search the answer, it's the wrong question). We can't blame learners for using the internet for what it was designed for—information gathering. Our challenge is finding ways to create worthy work (causes) that will push students to work towards open-ended solutions.

Some of us remember looking up things in encyclopedias. They gave us insight into a set of limited topics with paragraphs of information. The need for those research skills has significantly been eliminated with devices that allow you to perform searches with images, songs, bird calls, and even colors. Think of the exponential leap researching has taken now that you can simply press a button in your music app while a song is playing and the names of the song and the artist will appear. All this from a device that fits in your pocket.

What does this have to do with learning? Very little. It may serve a small part of the learning journey, but the answers we get from internet searches are for questions that have very little to do with real learning. If these are the answers we are looking for in the classroom, then we are asking the wrong questions.

We should help students learn how to navigate digital and non-digital resources and determine which is better in different situations. They have to know how to be great at giving interviews and how to steer conversations to get the answers that will help them in their journey.

We need them to be inventive and find creative ways to apply this research to their real challenges.

These revolution@ry learners are living in an age where the voice search feature on an app gives the answer to questions we would have previously viewed as being a part of learning or doing "real work." We need to rethink how learners put everything together.

This change provides a tremendous opportunity for leaders who commit to the revolution.

Communicators

We said this earlier, but we don't need adults to be the sage on the stage—we need learners to tell the story. We have to help learners organize and deliver talking points to their audience.

Are we allowing learners to present their findings?

Are we creating a stage to showcase what they have built?

Are we facilitating talks with outside agencies and people?

These are the real questions to present when we reflect on how we are preparing learners for tomorrow.

In Action

We wanted to share some stories of revolution@ry teachers in our schools who have taken the reins and have led significant change in their areas:

- Angie Plaine (@angieplaine) is a sixth-grade science teacher at HSMS. During the winter and spring of 2017, learners in her room designed and researched learning activities that focused on the plastic pollution problem prevalent in our world today. She had to utilize two classrooms to accommodate all the activities. In her room, students presented their findings and talked about what they wanted to research further. One young lady, after her presentation, broke the class up into groups of three and led them through a sorting activity. In the empty classroom next door, four student groups conducted experiments with plastics samples. They measured their density and classified them based on whether they floated or sank in salt water. They did all this to add to conversations about how harmful different kinds of plastic are to sea life.

- Lori Rabon (@rabonlb) implemented an interesting PBL with the medical field. She designed an exploration that has students assume the roles of doctors, hospital social workers, and other professionals and gives them a problem involving four people who need a heart transplant with different conditions. Students have to explore what each professional's role would be in the process of determining where the heart should go. What would instructional design look like if we focused on the conversations and decisions professionals have to make and allowed our students to interview them instead of reading about a career profile off the internet? This activity produced curiosity, so now, if students are so inclined, they can begin researching what they need to do to get into that field.

These real-life learning experiences clearly connect to Barbara Bray's reflections earlier. She also notes the following:

> Student agency is a must. Students have to have voice and input in determining their own learning trajectory. Empowering students with the autonomy of open research headed towards a specific goal prepares them to persevere through unknown challenges and eliminates (or reduces) the

learned helplessness that has been embedded in our tradi-
tional learning system. Instead of being told what to do and
how to learn, students as independent, self-directed learners
can be challenged and empowered with the tools, freedom
and support needed to achieve learning goals and targets.

REVOLUTION@ARY IDEA

Passion is fed from a curious mind, not the information on a sheet.

Myths about Revolution@ry Learners

The journey towards empowerment and student agency can seem scary. Obviously there is a transfer of some power, but this is part of the process of rethinking our perception of control in order to gain more buy-in and create curiosity in our learners. This is part of re-imagining learning environments. With this move comes concerns about what the "new" will look like. It's easy to imagine the worst about our learners, but the truth is this happens in classrooms and schools every day.

We're going to address some common misconceptions about revolution@ry learning below:

1. There is no accountability.

Learners are held to higher standards. Instead of merely looking at grades, we are also requiring them to manage time, conversations, planning, and what they create. Regarding grades, instead of using the outdated measures of giving As, Cs and Ds on a deadline, we embrace our role as facilitators and build benchmarks for progress monitoring, reflection, and adjustments to reach the final goal.

2. Students will run wild.

As we continue to say, we build up culture in learning environments and shift away from the role of rules enforcer. High expectations are taught, modeled, and retaught as needed. Revolution@ry learners follow the standards set by revolution@ry leaders!

3. There is not a focus on academics.

The examples we've provided have all been real experiences of teachers who have rethought how standards are taught, made content high interest, and empowered students to dive deep into research, problem solving and demonstrating their understanding and mastery.

4. Pandemonium will ensue.

Let's shift our goal from a quiet classroom to an active learning environment. Again, build the culture you want in your learning environment. What are teacher and learner actions when there is a call for quiet or when we are in groups? From hand signals to environment norms, everything should be planned carefully and taught repeatedly.

5. Teachers are not needed.

Revolution@ries know they are needed. Learners will always need guidance, wisdom, and encouragement to keep moving forward! Your role may shift to facilitator, but that's good for everyone.

6. Technology is a must.

Technology is liberating and provides options, but it is a component, not the mainstay. Compelling work drives real learning.

CALL TO ACTION

▶ With a revolution@ry partner on your grade level, team, or department, take a look at opportunities for students to demonstrate learning (in class, on grade level, and school) and broaden that scope.

▶ Create standards for communication and research for your learners and share them with your community.

▶ Plan a Maker Faire, TED Talk, or celebration of learning for your school.

CHAPTER 9

REVOLUTION@RY LEADERS

IN A SCHOOL SETTING, everyone—principal, teacher, parent, cafeteria manager, technology specialist—plays a key role in establishing a collective purpose and growth mindset. It's hard work, and it can't fall to just one person or just one group of people. It takes many hands. It also takes revolution@ry leaders—and we're not just talking about titles here—who are willing to deviate from the norm, the status quo, the way it's always been done. This kind of work requires open-minded leaders who will provide flexible environments to grow and educate kids. Flexible environments produce flexible teachers, and flexible teachers encourage flexible thinking in the classroom.

REVOLUTION@ARY IDEA

Flexible Environments + Flexible Teachers = Flexible Thinkers

Being a revolution@ry leader at any school level isn't easy. It can result in criticism, division, doubt, or even outright ridicule. But it can also yield astounding personal and academic growth among students and teachers alike.

Throughout our careers, we have observed and learned from a long and distinguished list of leaders. Incorporating the lessons we've learned from them and our own hopes for the future, we have narrowed down what it means to be a revolution@ry leader. These characteristics have parallels to the mindsets in chapter 2. Revolution@ry leaders are a complex lot. They learn from failure and build relationships. They are compassionate. They are visionary yet grounded. They are bold yet reflective.

Learning from Failure

"How are you able to make this change or paradigm shift?" is a common question we receive. First, we are very fortunate to have superintendents who have a clear vision for a new kind of learning. Superintendent Jim Holbeck (Harrisburg) gives me (Darren) flexibility to reinvent education. His direction influences our processes in my building. Then, the goal is for the leader in the classroom to provide the same flow to learners.

Our view of failure has a realness to it. We answer to several levels of stakeholders in our work. Failure hurts. It's messy, and it creates tension. Revolution@ry leaders embrace failure, even when it is hard, as a learning opportunity instead of a negative consequence that should be avoided.

The best example of this for the Harrisburg School District has been our personalized/customized learning initiative. For a state that is deeply conservative in educational values, moving to a new educational model of learning was a big risk. Mr. Holbeck understood our kids needed this change in a changing world. We wanted our kids to own their learning through this model. Was this change difficult? Absolutely. We dealt with skeptics. We dealt with angry parents. Some of the comments were harsh. There was real pain from real people.

Leaders in our district had to listen to the struggles and issues to understand how to make corrections. Failure didn't lead to quitting. The key to our perseverance was a group of leaders, administrators, and teachers, who understood that failure and learning from our mistakes produces a better quality education. There have been and continue to be challenges in our personalized learning model, but fear of not trying outweighed the fear of failure for the educators in our district. Our kids deserve more from us, and creating change requires a growth mindset and flexible environments of learning.

Committing to empowering educators with flexibility is a powerful gift and tool. It sends a clear message of trust and support. Flexibility in the classroom can give rise to innovative thoughts and actions among learners and educators. When the central office and building administrator give teachers the freedom to modify their work, kids benefit. They grow in their learning. Educators must be free to make decisions for their learners—even when failure is a real possibility—for the overall learning process to evolve.

Building Relationships

We all know the importance of building relationships in our profession. We are all leaders: central office, building level, and classroom leaders. How well we create our relationship structure results in positive or negative outcomes. In Harrisburg, South Dakota, culture is built before kids enter our buildings. Superintendent Jim Holbeck started a district culture-building theme when he began his role there. It is built on providing certified and classified staff with an enjoyable and entertaining experience during in-service. Can I use the word "fun" here? He wants our time together to be fun. The most recent example was when he used the theme "The Tonight Show This Morning" for our time together. On stage we had a group of educators replicating a band format on a late-night talk show. There was a host, another staff person, who guided conversations with "guests" from the district and outside the district. The guests from our district highlighted initiatives in our schools, while those outside the district talked about valuing kids. Jim Holbeck even brought in a special guest in 2018, the producer of the movie Napoleon Dynamite, Sean Covel. Sean is a native South Dakotan, which facilitated the connection, but his message inspired all the staff to right their compass for kids to begin the year.

Revolution@ry Relationship with Parents

Stephen Santilli (@SPSantilli) is an Assistant Superintendent in New Jersey. Stephen is best known for taking the Edcamp movement for educators and providing a similar format for parents. He has discovered one way to make his district transparent for his parents. His ParentCamp allows parents to ask questions and learn about their school. It is also structured to include everyone as an expert. He has some insight regarding communication with parents:

BOOST PARENT INVOLVEMENT WITH PARENTCAMP
BY REVOLUTION@RY LEADER
STEPHEN SANTILLI (@SPSANTILLI)

The Edcamp model focuses on a true "unconference." Therefore sessions are created the morning of the event and conversations are guided or facilitated by those generating the session. However the most important part of the unconference model is the idea of having session facilitators rather than presenters, which supports the notion that everyone in the room is the expert and has something to contribute, rather than just one person. With that model in mind, ParentCamp was born. While I did not organize the very first ParentCamp, I did collaborate with those who did. The resources they shared, as well as sharing what worked and didn't work, were invaluable and led to the success of future ParentCamps in our school/district.

Start Small: We first attempted a ParentCamp, or unconference for parents, through our normal Parent Involvement Committee (PIC) Meeting. This meeting allowed for approximately two hours of time to work with. Rather than generating sessions on the spot, we pre-determined approximately four sessions with in-district and out-of-district facilitators on a variety of topics. This allowed us to share resources with parents while giving them an option of what they were going to attend. We had approximately fifty minutes, which allowed for two sessions to occur with transition time.

After receiving positive feedback from the smaller unconference format, we planned for a larger event. A team was developed which consisted of staff and parents who shared the responsibilities in planning the event. Unlike an Edcamp, ParentCamp starts with a keynote. We have found success with keynotes that range from thirty to forty minutes. This allows parents the opportunity to gain a focus for the day as well as receive information on a broader topic. Also unlike an Edcamp, the sessions are not built the morning of the event. It is important for parents to know what they might be participating in prior to the event, especially since we held our first ParentCamp on a Saturday from approximately 8:00 a.m. to 12:30 p.m. The sessions again focused on a variety of topics that could meet the needs of elementary and secondary parents and utilized both facilitators from our own staff and experts in the community. A unique aspect of this conference is that students can also facilitate sessions, and one middle school student even facilitated a session on MineCraft for our parents. The model we use for ParentCamp is in essence a hybrid of the Edcamp model, but it allows for important face-to-face interaction with parents and provides them with valuable resources to meet the needs of their own children.

Visionary Yet Grounded

With the support of leaders who share this vision, change can be accelerated. We spoke earlier of developing a collective purpose for the school. A great vision, no matter how noble, grand, or practical, won't survive unless a unified vision is built and good support through planning and training is put in place.

We started our creative efforts for change with an examination of what learners need to be future-ready. This can be a bold departure from traditional academic goals because people have difficulty replacing the traditional three Rs with a focus on the revolution@ry characteristics we described earlier. It takes bold vision to see that and plan for it, but we also have to stay grounded and keep the total academic needs and goals of the school in mind.

I (Derek) changed school systems so I could be closer to home and family. Once I made the decision, I hoped to find a school that really needed me, where I could serve to help learners and the community. I was fortunate to find a home in Grady County Schools

(@gradycoschools). Dr. Kermit Gilliard shared with me a great "vision-ary yet grounded" talk: "We have to move from where we are to where we can be because our students need us to do more." We discussed our need to gradually and steadily move our staff and community.

In one of our first talks here at Washington Middle, the staff was very enthusiastic about changing our approach to managing how stu-dents behave (compliance) to outlining values we want our learners to have when they leave us. If you're in a small community like ours, you know the reality of students leaving and coming back to the area or starting their work lives soon after school. It makes it imperative to instill values we want to see in our learners at an early age. We've talked about them with our students and parents as well, to bring in all voices and input. We created Tiger V.O.I.C.E.:

VALUE
OWNERSHIP
INTEGRITY
COMPASSION
EMPATHY

This wasn't just change for the sake of change—the Tiger Family saw a better way to build a vision that will serve our school.

Bold Yet Reflective

Envisioning what is next is a powerful gift and opportunity. It also bears the responsibility of seeing it through. It can unify or cause division. This is the weight of leadership, at whatever level you serve. How you choose to make it happen, though, is the test of real leadership.

The typical impression of a bold leader is someone with a bullish nature who is independent and doesn't account for people working around them. Leaders like this do exist, but revolution@ry leaders have a boldness that purposefully brings others into the vision or initiative. They accept feedback and reflect. Reflecting on our work might be the most critical quality for professional growth and school learning.

We have to throw in our thoughts on limitations to a network in our school.

Launch a mutiny against these limitations. How open is your district to using social media? In the fall of 2017, EdSurge quoted a few of our thoughts regarding this topic. (Follow the QR code to the article.) Whatever your level of use at your school, you have to agree that our kids  need to be taught appropriate use of social media. The problem is that kids are receiving devices without any support or counsel on how to use them with digital citizenship and literacy in mind.

At HSMS we have opened up platforms like Facebook to our kids during certain time frames for instructional purposes. When our eighth graders were working on a project with Bergen, Norway, Facebook Groups was our platform to house the comments regarding discrimination and prejudice of native peoples for our kids. Kids could learn and discuss issues related to Native Americans and the Sami of

Norway. Some teachers have even accepted learning artifacts from Instagram accounts as evidence of learning. Most of you are probably thinking, "There is no way that can happen in my classroom or school." How long will we live in fear?

REVOLUTION@ARY IDEA

**We cannot be governed by fear.
We must keep learning as the priority.**

Fear is real, but so is teaching our expectations and modeling desired behaviors. Remember: we build the culture we want.

Compassionate

Change is hard, but it is manageable when you have people around you that display compassion. Pull apart the word compassion. Com means "with," while passion means "to suffer." If you display compassion, you suffer with others. When you are creating revolution@ry change, it helps to have others around you with a compassionate heart.

Significant change is relative—what's profound to one person or group may not be as big a leap to another. And when you take into account someone else's beliefs and foundation, it can be an overwhelming experience when we agree to change. At WRMS, introducing deeper implementation of blended learning meant changing up professional development for teachers and embracing being coaches more than administrators. Even with great support, it was hard to see more changes in classrooms. Remembering that we work with real people is a critical part of our work.

Being compassionate and understanding that we have to support change as much as we lead it by serving the real people who work in our school helps us make change lasting and sustainable. Real people have real need and feelings that must be addressed throughout any change. Seeing people and their needs is priority one.

Leading with Grit

If we had you describe the qualities of a leader, the list would be large and diverse. But being a leader isn't as much about qualities to possess as it is about a philosophy to follow. One of my (Darren) favorite quotes is, "The speed of the leader is the speed of the team." What is your speed within your school or classroom? Speed refers to the movement of progressive initiatives. It requires an attitude of grit. This has less to do with working hard and more to do with building capacity for change.

There is one quality that comes to mind for us in our work to change the outdated processes of education. If you want to lead a revolution, you need to be a risk-taker. When someone asks you for the research behind your "crazy" idea, you respond by telling them you can't wait for the research to come out two or three years in the future when you are seeing the immediate results now.

Administrators need to model flexibility for their staff. It is similar to the implementation of technology—the initiative is more effective when the leaders are using and modeling the technology. Flexibility is the same. If you want flexible thinkers, you need flexible teachers. If you want flexible teachers, administrators must build and protect a flexible environment that promotes risk-taking.

When you see the value of taking risks, the door opens for innovation. Risk-taking is not innate for everyone, and very few educators will take risks in a closed, rigid environment. How do you encourage someone to take risks? Modeling can help, but many people need more of a push to action. Leaders will need to find moments to place people in risky environments. Those who are resistant to leaving the status quo will be very uncomfortable, so why would we push them? Because we believe our learners are worth the risk. It all comes back to our kids in our classrooms and schools.

CALL TO ACTION

▶ How can school and district leaders empower teachers?

▶ How can teachers communicate their needs to administration?

▶ What are some of the pressing topics parents want to know about in elementary, middle, or high schools today?

▶ What other ways have you found to connect parents with the school or classroom?

CHAPTER 10

REVOLUTION@RY LEARNING

WHY DO ADULTS BELIEVE they need to make all the decisions in a child's learning? The voice of a kindergartener can be powerful and possess some much-needed childlike wisdom. The voice of a sixth grader can be powerful. The voice of a ninth grader can be powerful. Their voices SHOULD be powerful, so why are we holding them back from being heard? Too often we underestimate the value of their words because they are small, young, and immature. We hope this chapter will challenge you to open your mind to the voice of all your learners.

We both believe that learning should have a current vibe to it. The revolution@ries we admire most have created instructional pathways to learning that are on the leading edge of teaching. Many might argue that traditional instruction has produced good test results, and that's great if you want to produce students—or future employees—who are simply good test takers. But there is nothing about a standardized test that's the least bit empowering for a learner.

If you want to have students in your classroom, then keep teaching models from the twentieth century. If you want to have learners in your classroom, then keep reading this chapter. A lot in our culture and world has changed, but education continues to keep a vice-like grip on tradition. There are definitely some instructional practices that are still relevant, but our kids today are primed to be learners. They are looking to you to lead the revolution they need.

You can help revolutionize our craft by looking at the voice and choice you should provide to learners. Take a look at our personalized learning and iChoose models as a step toward learners advocating for themselves.

Learners

"Why do you call students learners?" This is a common question presented by educators and business professionals who are visiting HSMS. They are wondering what the difference is. We ask you this question: Do you want to be labeled a student or a learner? At the first glance, they appear to be similar, but there is a big difference in their meaning.

For decades we have called our kids students, and for us, the image of "students" involves this:

- sitting in rows of straight desks

- giving your attention to the teacher, who is standing at the front, for prolonged periods of time
- completing an assignment that has been used for the past ten years
- doing the same work as everyone else in the room, even though some kids are beyond the concept and others have not comprehended it yet

It is time to break this hypnotic hold on education. Learners hold tightly to the word "learn." It involves driving their education and being allowed to voice or make decisions that fit their...learning. Learners are empowered to manage their pathway and create experiences relevant to their talent. This is one example of a new way to learn.

At the National Principals Conference in 2017, I was awarded the National Digital Principal of the Year. I shared the stage with several other inspiring leaders and had 30 seconds to explain my passion in education. Penning these words was difficult given the limited amount of time, but it did force me to be concise. This focus led me to address not only the role of technology in K–12 education but also a continuum I feel is present. A majority of classrooms and schools fall into one of two categories: compliance and engagement. But there is a third category that is at a higher level than the other two, and that is empowerment.

I grew up in an educational system that relied on and demanded compliance. I played the game very well and was compliant with my teachers and the rote assignments they gave me. We still have many schools that cling to compliant cultures with a top-down approach to lesson delivery and management. What does this look like? It looks like a student who merely sits and takes in information from a teacher. It looks like a teacher assigning a consequence without conversation. It looks like a teacher who talks at a student instead of with a student.

The problem today is that fewer students want to play the game and are resisting a control-centered system. We have more and more students asking for a revolution. Are we listening? They have been born into an on-demand world where information, entertainment, and connection to the entire planet is at their fingertips. Is it fair or realistic to ask them to power down when they come to school? Powering down wasn't an option for us because we were never really powered (or empowered) up!

Engagement

Engagement has been used as a measurement of learning behavior...wait, let me take that back. It measures *on-task* behavior. If students are working quietly on a digital or print worksheet, is that considered high engagement? Whom does that serve—teacher or student? To be honest, this level of engagement feels good. It allows a student who just asks what they need to do to receive an "A." Many times it does not involve thinking critically. Kids say, "Just tell me what to do!"

REVOLUTION@ARY REFLECTION

Teachers are great at compliance— revolution@ries EMPOWER learners!

By the way, adults are not much different from kids. When we speak at conferences, it feels good to see adults engaged, listening to the message, but adults are often just like kids. They are checking email, texting, or on social media instead of engaging with the material. So the reflection question for you is, are you engaged *or* are you not taking advantage of your opportunity to be empowered in your own learning and growth?

Are You Ready to Empower?

We wanted the third level, empowered, to be the spearhead for this chapter. It fuels our belief in personalized learning and other empowered programs. At first this book had the word empowered in the main title because we are moving our teachers and students toward a focus on empowerment. What visuals come to mind when you reflect on the word empowered? For me it is a driver's ed car. Driver's education students work their way from the back seat to the front passenger seat to the driver's

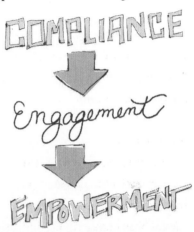

seat. They are empowered to take the wheel after some driver training. Empowering those students does not mean a loss of control for the instructor. Who is sitting in the passenger seat during driver's ed? The driver's ed instructor. The instructor provides guidance as needed. The instructor also has access to a brake and will apply pressure as necessary for protection while the students are learning. The instructor also provides feedback.

When learners are empowered to drive their learning, they are provided voice and choice in their learning pathway. Kids have a sense of pride in the ownership they acquire from this empowerment. This is their education, and they need to be able to make decisions on pathways, rubrics, assignments, feedback, etc. Turn the wheel over to them, and you will be surprised by their growth.

Voice and Choice: Team Innovate

A few years ago, Mary Perrine (@Learningosity) shared a personalized learning model with our staff. I had always wanted our kids to have more choice in their learning but couldn't find the right fit. When Mary and her team began talking, it was an instant "aha" moment. She graciously helped us through the ups and downs of change until we made it our own. We called the group "Team Innovate."

The term "personalized learning" conjures up many possible definitions and thoughts. I visit with many people who view technology and software as the driver for personalized learning, but in my opinion they are missing the golden buzzer of learning in education. They put technology on the field of learning and leave the kids on the sideline waiting to get in the game. I believe personalized learning is the reverse. It is the LEARNER leading the voice and choice charge with technology waiting on the sideline to enhance and transform the ideas from the kids. Kids are always first.

Team Innovate is based on a cohort model that utilizes facilitators from the four core subjects of math, social studies, English-language arts, and science. Teachers from these four subject areas discuss how they can meet a variety of learner needs on a daily basis. Before they discuss content, however, they spend time creating culture. As a matter of fact, there is no content in the first two to four weeks. (Some groups take even more time.) What are they doing? They're team building, taking learning inventories, creating norms or standard operating procedures (SOPs), doing growth mindset activities, and understanding the language of learning and advocacy. We are working to develop a family culture.

The voice and choice come in the offerings, or learning opportunities, developed by facilitators (teachers). Facilitators create offerings based on the learning pathways of their learners. These offerings are not always the same for each offering, or period, each day. It is common that a science facilitator will have two or three unique offerings. Having a variety of offerings allows facilitators to meet the needs of more learners. Traditionally we teach a lesson to all twenty-five students in a room whether they need it or not, whether they can handle it or not. Personalized learning at HSMS provides more choice. How do facilitators know what to offer? They receive feedback from the kids and repeat or create new offerings based on need.

I like to say, "This is where the magic happens!" There are over seventy sixth graders on the floor in one room. Learners are viewing the offerings from the four facilitators. The offerings vary in structure, pacing, and choice. Voice and choice in learning are high priorities at HSMS, but this model of personalized learning allows learners to create their schedule on a daily basis. Eleven- and twelve-year-olds schedule their learning on a daily basis. They do not have a static schedule handed to them at the start of the year that tells them where to go and when to be there. These learners measure their learning choices with thoughtfulness and intentionality. They do what is best for their learning.

This cohort of four facilitators provides offerings that meet the needs of most, if not all, learners. After each facilitator finishes their explanation of the offering in a block of time, there is a "dance," a give-and-take with the learners who ask questions and negotiate present and future offerings. They also navigate or find holes in the puzzle created by our facilitators. Learners approach this with an attitude of, "How are you going to meet my needs in my learning?" This concept is so foreign in our educational system today that you often have to see it to understand it. You can see examples on my YouTube Channel (Darren Ellwein).

The learners then choose their offerings for each content area based on what is best for them in a particular content area. Our cohorts have also learned to collaborate on mastery projects. Science and ELA use their standards on one piece of mastery (one project that meets standards in both content areas).

A simple slide captures the learning opportunities offered for a day. Facilitators have started to include simple innovations and visual hooks such as GIFs, emojis, and catchy titles that make the learners ponder what they will experience in the offering. Learners hear all the possible offerings from four facilitators, make sense of the puzzle pieces in their schedule, and create their own pathway. Learners have led offerings as well. "Zach Attack" was an example of a learner-led offering about reptiles (see 10.2). I would have to write another book to explain the learner language of the coding used in these images. Flex, MT, and iLearn are signposts for our kids in their learning journey.

Time	Mrs. Plaine	Mrs. Long	Mr. Klumper	Mr. Donnelly
A	LT 3 Earth Layers Coaching Workshop	**Literature Circle** Preparation Meeting #3: Thursday	LT6 iLearn Meng Jiangnu's Tears	Wednesday, January 17th Attendance Code: A52F
B	SWAT the FLY SLO & midpoint QUIZ	**FLEX** Lit. Circle- read & role Gravana 1.6	LT6 iLearn Meng Jiangnu's Tears	EMERGENCY! MT 3 COACHING WORKSHOP
C	SWAT the FLY SLO & midpoint QUIZ	**FLEX** Lit. Circle- read & role Gravana 1.6	LT6 iLearn Meng Jiangnu's Tears	READY FOR MT 3 REVIEW – NOT READY FOR MASTERY
D	SWAT the FLY SLO & midpoint QUIZ	**Literature Circle** Preparation Meeting #3: Thursday	LT6 iLearn Who were the BUILDERS?	Ready for MT 3 Mastery

Time	Mrs. Plaine	Mrs. Long	Mr. Klumper	Mr. Donnelly
A	STOP SUCKING.	*Watsons Mastery* Prewrite & First Draft	Creatively Comparing Governments Finding similarities and differences	Monday, March 26th BRING IN GALLON MILK/JUICE BOTTLES!
B	ZACH ATTACK!	*Watsons Mastery* Prewrite & First Draft	Creatively Comparing Governments Finding similarities and differences	15.1 PERSONAL FLEX/SEMINAR
C	Could MY straw make it to a GYRE?	*Watsons Mastery* **Socratic Seminar:** Make Up (5)	Creatively Comparing Governments Finding similarities and differences	MT 3 MASTERY MAKEUP
D	STOP SUCKING.	Gravana 1.10: CW Locked In *Watsons Mastery* (5)	Creatively Comparing Governments Finding similarities and differences	MT 6 AHEAD OF PACE LEARNERS – NORWAY CONNECTION

As one HSMS parent noted to a group of principals at the 2018 National Principals Conference in Chicago, "My daughter, because of this personalized learning model, has better time management skills than most of the employees that work for me at my business. She didn't have these skills initially, but learning to advocate for herself grew them."

This community time, which includes scheduling their day, lasts twenty minutes or less. We use a social-emotional learning program called Habits of Mind (HoM) during the remaining minutes. For example, one month we will focus on a HoM related to thinking flexible or persisting. Many of our activities are now organically created by facilitators or our school counselor. We are very intentional about having learners tell stories related to the HoM. Parents have come to school asking why their child told them to "find humor" in their day or "persist" through their adult work. This is just another piece to the culture we are creating.

Personalized Learning in One Room

Single classrooms personalize in our building as well. One educator to highlight is Maria Pettinger, an English-language arts and Spanish instructor. She personalizes her content within her ELA studio (classroom). After several weeks of training learners in procedures and seeking their voice in norms and spaces, she slowly turns over the reins of her objectives to them. She provides a snapshot of learning opportunities and then releases them to form their learning needs within her room. Her learners either use her choices or create their own based on the learning targets. The learning spaces they create range from individual work time to collaborative zones to peer tutor areas. Maria then has one-on-one conferences designed to provide immediate and relative feedback to learners needing a push.

Maria trusts her learners and gives them freedom to change the learning environment. Depending on what they need for their learning, they will produce a floor plan, get approval, and redesign spaces. Maria recently had her learners brainstorm ideas for expository and persuasive writings. Kids used paper/pencil, iBooks, Popplet, and whiteboarding. Voice and choice in learning.

Check out this example of creativity and voice: One girl saw I was taking pictures of her brainstorming and emailed me her finished product (whiteboarding on our homemade tables and student desks). I told her that I was bummed I couldn't be there to record her explaining her work. The next day she sent me a video explaining her work. I didn't ask for the video, but she went home with her iPad, used the whiteboarding picture, made a green screen with a green t-shirt, placed the picture in iMovie, and explained the ideas with a voiceover in iMovie. It was brilliant! You can find this video on my (Darren's) YouTube Channel (goo.gl/UN5cLo).

How to Be Current

I am always gleaning ideas from different types of text or digital media. As I was watching *America's Got Talent* one night, I heard an interesting comment from one of the judges, who said the act that had just performed was "current." When that word registered with me, educators in my building and on my Twitter professional network came to mind. Think of those who are transforming learning with hacks of current tools or ideas and innovating the original concept or idea.

One example is Joe Klumper (@joeklumper), who wanted to produce a Snapchat experience for his learners while studying Paleolithic and Neolithic ages. Here are his words:

SNAP IT!
BY REVOLUTION@RY EDUCATOR
JOE KLUMPER (@JOEKLUMPER)

When many students enter school—be it each year, each day or each individual class period—they leave their world behind and slip into the comfortably-constructed environment built by their teachers. For teachers the most comfortable environment is one we are familiar with: phrases, tech tools, and strategies used repeatedly. However, this familiar world is not where students live and breathe. Our class rosters are mash-ups of online, digitally in-tune, and hard-to-entertain youth, no longer looking to their teacher for information—they can find that quickly online—but looking for someone who understands them and acknowledges their world. Using tools already in the hands of students to help them learn not only causes a quick "are you serious?" moment—that is just a bonus—but it also relays the message that you see and accept who they are and the things they already constantly use.

Enter Snapchat.

From banning phones to monitoring how they are being used, students hear a chorus of "no, no, no" in regard to the one device they cherish more than anything. Regardless of how hard it may be for us to understand the value our students place on what we often consider silly uses of technology, if we choose to embrace these tools rather than ban them, students are going to show us how badly they crave validation that their interests are accepted in school.

Snapchat. Snapchat.

The word Snap alone has been known to send chills down the spine of educators, not to mention using the crazy-filter, fleeting-picture messaging app in the classroom. When I introduced the idea to students, my excitement to use Snapchat was met with some of those "are you serious?" looks. So I answered them with a giddy "of course I am." Buy-in and engagement instantaneously maxed out, while all eyes locked in and none of those pesky side-conversations were taking place that every teacher grows frustrated with. I was hit with total focus because I was speaking their language, not the antiquated (from their perspective) language that everyone in my adult world speaks.

This can be phrased in any number of ways, but I can visualize teachers and students cohesively coming together when considering the idea of "meeting students where they're at." Rather than experience growing frustration over the students who give no effort, invest no energy, or accept no ownership of their education, perhaps we need only a change in how we utilize the tools students already use. Maybe the root cause of apathy in our classrooms is always expecting students to meet us and reside in their teacher's familiar world, rather than us meeting them where they are.

While students created Snaps of themselves living or visiting the Neolithic Stone Age, they were behaving and working like anyone would who is given freedom to use tools they are comfortable with and are reinforced by a tone of acceptance for who they are. Students possess such potential. When given the right opportunity, they will work harder than we may have thought possible. It might not be the only ingredient, but using tools in the classroom that students are already using in their daily lives can be a very powerful part of the recipe.

The use of Snapchat, or any other social media tool, can be done in a variety of ways. To work around internet restrictions and varying accessibility of students' personal devices, adjustments were made. Instead of using the real Snapchat app, we created Snapchat-designed photos with Pages, since all the students in our school have iPads. We have done the same in other situations to create Instagram and Twitter posts. As an added bonus to this entire process, the use of digital media design appeals to a certain portion of every student population. This would not have been necessary if the actual apps had been used.

Gamification

Justin Owens (@MrOwens_Math) has also done a deep dive with gamification in his classroom to not only bring personalized learning to his classroom but also to engage students on another level. He gives a good account of some efforts with gamification and the impact it can have in your classroom.

GAMIFICATION: WHAT IS IT?
BY REVOLUTION@RY EDUCATOR
JUSTIN OWENS (@MROWENS_MATH)

Gamification in education is actually a subcategory of Personalized Learning (PL), though it is certainly deserving of a chapter or book of its very own. Gamification is deeply rooted in PL.

In order to successfully implement gamification in the classroom, strong relationships with students is a must.

Personalized learning can seem very chaotic to those who are unfamiliar with it, so it is vital to be comfortable with releasing control and have solid expectations established in the classroom culture. The district I work in, Rowan-Salisbury Schools, and the school where I currently serve, West Rowan Middle School, have a strategic focus on personalized learning.

Gamification in the classroom is the process of using game mechanics in the design of classroom experiences in an effort to engage, empower, and elicit joy from students when completing a task. These mechanics can be taken from video games, board games, card games, deck building games, and more. The only real requirement here is drawing students into an experience where they will think deeply, work smarter, collaborate, and enjoy the process. In the table below, I have listed just a few of the game mechanics you might consider incorporating in your classroom, but this is by no means meant to be an exhaustive list.

Game Mechanics

Leaderboards	Boss Battles	Experience Points (XP)
Badges / Achieve-ments	Unlocking Powers	Leveling Up
Side Quest	Collaboration	Investigations
	Gold Points (GP)	

I understand what you're thinking: this all sounds vaguely exciting, but what does it actually look like? What is it useful for? Is it more than just a fun time for students? How do I get started? You've come to the right place. As I said above, my classroom is structured such that about 90 percent of what we do in the course is gamified in some manner. Let's Dive In!

Narrative

This section is geared towards getting students to buy in to the gamified classroom. I'm currently a seventh-grade teacher, but I taught sixth grade a couple years before moving up to seventh grade. In my experience, this can be more challenging the older your students are; however I have seen it used in high schools and even college courses, so it can be done successfully at all grade levels.

Narrative is a technique you can design at the beginning of the year and then develop it further or adjust it throughout the school year. It helps to get students to buy in to the gamified classroom. It is essentially the back story or universe that your classroom exists within. You might, for example, be on a space station in orbit around Mars that is about to attempt colonization, or perhaps you are adventurers in a magical world of wizards and dragons. Perhaps you are time travelers who ride in a repurposed refrigerator that whizzes through all of time and space. Whatever it may be or develop into is completely up to you and your students' imagination. Just make sure you connect, solve, research, and investigate your content along the way through the adventure.

This has been a huge portion of my course design that has evolved over the past couple years. I started out using leaderboards with teams and have continued to add elements to my course to the point where students now create their own characters and super powers that are unique to them. Now every topic we cover in 7th-grade math is wrapped around a story, adventure, or investigation.

Get your students engaged in the narrative by having them create characters they will "play" as when participating in the classroom activities. As you plan events in your narrative and curriculum, include their characters in those plans. Share an activity with them that includes their characters and watch the delight, excitement, and engagement skyrocket during that lesson.

Immersive Investigations

Immersive investigations are a particular offshoot of the narrative aspect of gamification. They allow you to create an experience for your students that immerses them into not only the topic but the scenario you have crafted for them as well. These scenarios incorporate many of the other elements of

PL, such as: choice, collaboration, student ownership, project-based learning, gamification, and mastery learning. A great way to facilitate these types of experiences is through the creation of Hyperdocs. If you are unfamiliar with what Hyperdocs are, then you can check out a great book written by Lisa Highfill, Kelly Hilton, and Sara Landis called *The Hyperdoc Handbook*.

The most recent use of these types of investigations in my class sent students on a secret mission, chasing after the research of a kidnapped scientist! They were given multiple avenues to choose from to pursue their objectives and multiple opportunities to report back on their findings to the Secretary of State through the Flipgrid site. At the end of their research, groups were tasked with either creating a video, a graphic novel, or a Lego Animation that demonstrated the group's mastery of the concept they chose to research.

Why Give a Quiz? Give a Boss Battle Instead!

Boss Battles are a great way to give an assessment. Whether you consider it informal or formal (I use them as quizzes), Boss Battles are a great way to engage students in doing their best work on an assessment. If you already incorporate the Narrative technique mentioned above, then the Boss Battle is a natural extension of the story's outcome. A Boss Battle is an opportunity for students to play a game in the classroom where they are not competing but rather collaborating to defeat a common foe or villain. There are a lot of resources, videos, and other examples that already exist out there for Boss Battles. Everyone has an interesting take on this idea and how to implement it. All that I have come across are interesting and fun to use. When I use a Boss Battle in the classroom, I usually make some changes or adaptations to try to improve the experience each time. I have worked with a great colleague the past two years who has challenged me to improve this technique each time either of us use it.

In my classroom Boss Battles take place at the end of a unit or after we have covered a cluster of topics that need to be assessed. You want to either create a villain or use an adversary from popular culture for the students to battle. The villain attacks the class by barraging them with questions covering the topic you are assessing. This can be done in teams, guilds, or groups, depending on what you call them.

After being presented with a question, students are given a certain amount of time (e.g., two minutes) to work out the problem and discuss with their group. When work time has expired, the villain chooses a student at random to attack who is responsible for answering the question. If they answer correctly, then the student is given a die to roll. The number the die lands on determines how many hit points they get to take off the villain's life bar. For example, if your villain has 75 HP (hitpoints) and the student rolls a five, then they take away five HP from the villain's life, leaving him with 70 HP!

If a student answers the question incorrectly, then there must be some type of consequence. This can be that the villain strikes back at the class in retaliation. He could burn their notes up with a flamethrower, meaning they can no longer access notes during the next round of the battle. Maybe the boss takes away the class's ability to talk to their teammates for a given round. There are all kinds of actions the villain can take, but the key here is to make the event as immersive as possible for students. The more interactive the battle is for them, the more engaged they are in doing their best work. They are taking a quiz without it feeling like a quiz.

While it serves as a quiz on the instructor's end of the event, it is a learning experience for the students. Where my teaching might not have been making a solid impact on some students, the boss battle allows students to work collaboratively as they teach one another and see new ways of approaching a problem.

Listening to group conversations is one of the most satisfying aspects of these battles.

What is the Impact?

There are numerous benefits to this style of teaching, like: increased engagement and participation; deeper exploration of content and academic extensions into real life applications; learning twenty-first-century skills such as communication, collaboration, digital literacy, and digital application. In my classroom the more gamification and PL techniques I incorporate, the more learning grows. What speaks to me most are the smiles, laughter, and excitement I see in a middle school math class!

These are significant learning shifts from the middle school instruction of five, ten, or twenty years ago! Implementing these innovative practices in classrooms without also changing how we measure learning is counterproductive. What good does it do to rethink social media in the classroom, like using SnapChat to explore the Neolithic Age, if we are still looking for ways to assign an A or D or an 85 to a student's exploration? And while smiles don't necessarily give us a gauge of where a student is on mastering a topic, they do give us the best indication that we are reaching and connecting with students. These real-world revolution@ry practices require a change in how we understand and approach grading.

If you take away the digital tools and look at the intention and purpose of both these teachers, you will realize what we do. If these were non-tech classrooms, these learning spaces would still look very different because these leaders are committed to learner-centered instruction.

We contacted a true revolution@ry, Rick Wormeli, and we are making our full conversation available for all here. Rick has set a standard for this level of shift-thinking regarding grading and bringing the student into the learning and growth conversation. From his time as a middle school teacher to now as an education thought leader, he has been a steady voice in changing how we think and practice.

Rick asks, "Are we creating active creators or passive consumers?"

Think of your classroom and grade level and school. How do you answer that question? How would your teachers/students/parents answer it? That answer matters!

- *Who owns the learning?*
- *Who will get bored the easiest?*
- *Who can communicate their needs better?*
- *Who is the doctor you want helping you 20 years down the road?*
- *Whom would you rather have as a pilot?*
- *IN WHICH COMMUNITY OF LEARNERS WOULD YOU RATHER BE THE LEADER?*

Isn't it time to change a system or practice in your classroom or school that has been about "Gotcha" or control (keeping students in their place). Rick speaks to "ethical, accurate, empowering assessment and grading," not the systems we have developed from two hundred years ago or what has been co-opted in this age of accountability.

REVOLUTION@ARY IDEA

Is how you are assessing students inspiring hope or hopelessness? Empowerment or powerlessness? Agency or lack of control?

Do students go through the motions or see an opportunity for growth?

Teachers can provide many gifts to students and families. We've all heard the expression, in some form or fashion, that we don't remember a particular lesson, but we remember how that teacher made us feel. When I've heard people talk on this, I've never really thought of the specific feeling I want students to have. While I want students to be happy and have fond memories, recently I've been determined to let my involvement in their life make them feel hopeful, uplifted, and valued. And this has to happen in every aspect of our learning environment.

- Why shouldn't a struggling student who is engaged in a project using social media in social studies exploration feel uplifted after a coaching session with a teacher?
- Why shouldn't a student doing well on a project in Ag class feel hope when he/she is pushed after a feedback talk from a teacher?
- Does every student feel valued when they get feedback in your classroom? They should.

Check out our full talk with Rick here! You are doing yourself, your class, your team, and your school a disservice if you don't listen to him talk about our perception of "laziness," tenacity, agency, self-efficacy, and the host of other things that will  get you to seriously rethink your thoughts and belief about work, grading/assessments, and, more importantly, the students at the center!

CALL TO ACTION

▶ How can you personalize your content to increase empowerment for your kids?

▶ What are the 'current' cultural themes of your learners today?

▶ How do you bring more voice and choice into your classroom or school?

▶ In what ways can you collaborate with colleagues to combine learning targets?

Share your ideas online and tag them #revoltLAP.

A FINAL CALL TO ACTION

YOUR JOURNEY THROUGH THIS book is complete, but the greater story is yet to be written—your story! We urge you to answer the call to be revolution@ry in your practice. Learners need you to be revolution@ry and allow them to drive their learning. It's exciting to talk about revolution, but a revolt against the status quo doesn't happen without action. The words on these pages have no meaning unless you put them into practice.

There is nothing like getting a glimpse of the future and adjusting the present in light of what you've seen. There is nothing like using a vision of the future to help you get a jump on the challenges of tomorrow. It's a great feeling, and it's exciting to watch.

We've glimpsed the future of education. We have seen it through our learners and staff. We believe in all that it can be.

Our kids need us to always dream about a better tomorrow. It's how our country came to be. While I was visiting Derek on one of our writing weekends in Atlanta, we passed the exit for the Dr. Martin Luther King, Jr. Museum. It struck me how bold his convictions were. Bold to the point of losing his life for a cause. Bold enough to bring a revolution regarding a major social issue. He didn't wait for someone to inspire him. Dr. Martin Luther King, Jr. knew he had to empower people with his words and action. How bold are you being to bring change in education?

We need to spark a better today for our kids. A better today is influenced by revolution@ry dreams! The dreams in this book are reality, not fiction! The incredible teachers in our buildings are helping to paint a new landscape. These revolutions are taking place in small pockets across our country at elementary schools, middle schools, and high schools. We need to come together for a change that allows the educational dreams of kids to be reality.

Every change agent, every champion, was a middle school learner at one point. Our greatest strengths and opportunities don't lie in creating rigid systems wherein our goal is managing learners. Real success comes about when we are involving students in the choices and designs of learning experiences. This is the difference between inclusive leadership and exclusive management.

When we were in school, we can remember being told what to do, where and when to go, and how well to do it. In those days differentiation was accepting (or, in some cases, predetermining) which students would make As and which would sit in certain areas. Today, we can do better!

If we had some simple strategies to implement, they would be:

- Taking on new challenges with a positive mindset
- Stay away from what I call "door closers," people who respond with "no" or "you can't do that"
- Complimenting colleagues on risk-taking and their revolution@ry work
- Placing "Pushers" in your life
- Persisting through criticism
- Being willing to try
- Embracing vulnerability and fear and the value of risk (learners deserve it)

Be the revolution@ries our students need! Creating the culture and environment our learners need versus the one we experienced takes a bold acceptance that education methods must change. Being a revolution@ry just might change your relationship to the work you do. Make the decision to start a learner-empowered shift in your school. If we want learners to share and create, we have to help build that. If we want their choice to be an integral part of their learning, we have to let go of some of our thinking. And we can do it. Don't try it alone. Embrace this network.

Be revolution@ry.

Create revolution@ries.

#revoltLAP

BIBLIOGRAPHY

Chapter 2
Sheniger, Eric C. and Thomas C. Murray. *Learning Transformed: 8 Keys to Designing Tomorrow's Schools, Today* (Alexandria, Virginia: ASCD, 2017).

Chapter 3
Barrett, Peter, Fay Davies, Yufan Zhang, and Lucinda Barrett. "The Holistic Impact of Classroom Spaces on Learning in Specific Subjects." *Environment and Behavior*, May 2017; 49 (4); 425–451. ncbi.nlm.nih.gov/pmc/articles/PMC5394432.

Chapter 4
Tabaka, Marla. "Richard Branson's 10 Favorite Quotes on Collaboration." *Inc.com*, July 24, 2017, inc.com/marla-tabaka/virgins-success-is-driven-by-people-working-togeth.html.

Chapter 6

Mehta, R, Zhu, R and Cheema. "Is noise always bad? Exploring the effects of ambient noise on creative cognition," *Journal of Consumer Research*, 39, 784–99.

Chapter 7

Ellwein, D. "Creating a Maker Culture at Your School." *Principal Leadership*, April 2018; 24-25.

MORE FROM

Since 2012, DBCI has been publishing books that inspire and equip educators to be their best. For more information on our DBCI titles or to purchase bulk orders for your school, district, or book study, visit DaveBurgessconsulting.com/DBCIbooks.

More from the PIRATE™ Series

Teach Like a PIRATE by Dave Burgess

eXPlore Like a Pirate by Michael Matera

Learn Like a Pirate by Paul Solarz

Play Like a Pirate by Quinn Rollins

Run Like a Pirate by Adam Welcome

Lead Like a PIRATE™ Series

Lead Like a PIRATE by Shelley Burgess and Beth Houf

Balance Like a Pirate by Jessica Cabeen, Jessica Johnson, and Sarah Johnson

Lead beyond Your Title by Nili Bartley

Lead with Culture by Jay Billy

Lead with Literacy by Mandy Ellis

Leadership & School Culture

Culturize by Jimmy Casas

Escaping the School Leader's Dunk Tank by Rebecca Coda and Rick Jetter

From Teacher to Leader by Starr Sackstein

The Innovator's Mindset by George Couros

Kids Deserve It! by Todd Nesloney and Adam Welcome

Let Them Speak by Rebecca Coda and Rick Jetter

The Limitless School by Abe Hege and Adam Dovico

The Pepper Effect by Sean Gaillard

The Principled Principal by Jeffrey Zoul and Anthony McConnell

The Secret Solution by Todd Whitaker, Sam Miller, and Ryan Donlan

Start. Right. Now. by Todd Whitaker, Jeffrey Zoul, and Jimmy Casas

Stop. Right. Now. by Jimmy Casas and Jeffrey Zoul

Unmapped Potential by Julie Hasson and Missy Lennard

They Call Me "Mr. De" by Frank DeAngelis

Your School Rocks by Ryan McLane and Eric Lowe

Technology & Tools

50 Things You Can Do with Google Classroom by Alice Keeler and Libbi Miller

50 Things to Go Further with Google Classroom by Alice Keeler and Libbi Miller

140 Twitter Tips for Educators by Brad Currie, Billy Krakower, and Scott Rocco

Block Breaker by Brian Aspinall

Code Breaker by Brian Aspinall

Google Apps for Littles by Christine Pinto and Alice Keeler

Master the Media by Julie Smith

Shake Up Learning by Kasey Bell

Social LEADia by Jennifer Casa-Todd

Teaching Math with Google Apps by Alice Keeler and Diana Herrington

Teaching Methods & Materials

All 4s and 5s by Andrew Sharos

Ditch That Homework by Matt Miller and Alice Keeler

Ditch That Textbook by Matt Miller

Educated by Design by Michael Cohen, The Tech Rabbi

The EduProtocol Field Guide by Marlena Hebern and Jon Corippo

Instant Relevance by Denis Sheeran

LAUNCH by John Spencer and A.J. Juliani

Make Learning MAGICAL by Tisha Richmond

Pure Genius by Don Wettrick

Shift This! by Joy Kirr

Spark Learning by Ramsey Musallam

Sparks in the Dark by Travis Crowder and Todd Nesloney

Table Talk Math by John Stevens

The Classroom Chef by John Stevens and Matt Vaudrey

The Wild Card by Hope and Wade King

The Writing on the Classroom Wall by Steve Wyborney

Inspiration, Professional Growth & Personal Development

The Four O'Clock Faculty by Rich Czyz

Be REAL by Tara Martin

Be the One for Kids by Ryan Sheehy

Creatively Productive by Lisa Johnson

The EduNinja Mindset by Jennifer Burdis

How Much Water do We Have? by Pete and Kris Nunweiler

P Is for Pirate by Dave and Shelley Burgess

A Passion for Kindness by Tamara Letter

The Path to Serendipity by Allyson Apsey

Sanctuaries by Dan Tricarico

Shattering the Perfect Teacher Myth by Aaron Hogan

Stories from Webb by Todd Nesloney

Talk to Me by Kim Bearden

The Zen Teacher by Dan Tricarico

Children's Books

Dolphins in Trees by Aaron Polansky

The Princes of Serendip by Allyson Apsey

ABOUT THE AUTHORS

DARREN ELLWEIN is blessed to be the principal of Harrisburg South Middle School in Harrisburg, South Dakota. In 2017, he was awarded Digital Principal of the Year by the National Association of Secondary Principals, NASSP. He is an author, speaker, and consultant. He believes in empowering adults and kids to produce authentic learning experiences. His building and staff have embraced a maker culture and personalized learning environment. He has presented on various topics: leadership, personalized learning, makerspaces, design thinking, social media for professional growth and school promotion, innovative spaces and seating, and connecting with schools globally to transform learning.

DEREK MCCOY is the proud principal of Washington Middle School in
Grady County Schools. His focus is
on improving student learning and
achievement, increasing teaching effi-
cacy, and creating a learning environment that will prepare students for
their futures. His approach involves
innovative instructional design/best
practices as well as developing and
implementing relevant, student-cen-

tered, and flexible learning practices. He brings a wide range of expe-
riences as a secondary school assistant principal, instructional coach,
director of curriculum and innovation, and principal. In 2013, he was
named one of twenty-five educators to follow on Twitter by #NCED
and the Innovative School Partners. He was recognized as a 2014
Digital Principal of the Year by NASSP and has received recognitions
from other groups for his efforts to use social media and technology to
help connect learners with best practices and experts, create impactful
collaboration networks, and ultimately help grow all schools.

Made in the USA
Lexington, KY
26 April 2019